TSTW

Tara Saved The World

By Kevin Hugh Klassen

Foreword

I would like to dedicate this book to my one true love, planet Earth. You will never see me behind a podium shouting about climate change, I am not an activist. I am writing this book not to tell you what to do, you shouldn't feel pressure or guilt when you read this story. The climate is first on my most important list, it should be our first priority over everything because it threatens our very existence. This is not a typical book, I am not your typical writer; there are a few anomalies I did purposely, I hope you are entertained.

Tara Saved The World

Chapter One
The Evil Men Do

It was shortly before midnight on February 17, 2000, in Calgary, Alberta, a cold, wet night. Tara was working her second job, the late shift in a sandwich shop, she was working hard to save money to go back to school. A man in his early 30s, entered carrying a sledgehammer, he needed cash for some Crack. Tara did not give it to him.

Tara was my girlfriend's best friend, and I got to know her a little. I would describe Tara as a gentle spirit; she had a naive innocence about her, and when it came to her friends, she was fiercely loyal. In a way, she was broken and fragile. When Tara was young, an accident at home left a significant portion of her body scarred from being burned. I think she couldn't help being a bit self-conscious about the scarring, but she still had an extremely positive outlook on life.

We played games when she came over, had drinks, laughed, mostly, we played drinking games. There was this one time during a game of scrabble that sticks out in my mind. Nearing the end of the game, I placed my tiles on the board and played the word dolt. She smiled and asked if that was a real word; I reminded her that if she challenges me, she will lose her turn. I was coy with her, baiting her to do it. We were all smiling and laughing at the implication of challenging such a word. Finally, she decided to do it, so I looked it up in the dictionary and showed it to her. When she saw it, she smiled and shrugged it off as no big deal. She was there to hang with her best friend, and she was only mildly interested in the games that we played.

Tara and my girlfriend talked on the phone every day, sometimes for hours. They had previously worked together, and Tara even moved in with her when Tara was having problems at home. My girlfriend had helped her through some rough times, and now they shared a deep bond. They loved each other like sisters or like a mother and daughter.

Tara moved to a new apartment and desperately wanted us to come and check it out, and get hammered. When those two got together, it would almost always guarantee an evening of heavy drinking. Calgary is quite spread out, and Tara lived on the other side of town; we took the C-train there, the trip took over an hour. By the time we got to the last stop, I was urgently in need of a bathroom. I decided going in some nearby shrubs was better than going in my pants. I shouldn't have had those two beers before I left the house. Unfortunately for my girlfriend, who also had two beers before we left, she couldn't do what I did, there was a mad dash to Tara's apartment. When we got there, my girlfriend used the bathroom, and I tried to convince Tara that I may have urinated on her landlord's car. She didn't believe me for a second, she just smiled and added a ha-ha. She told me to have a seat at the already set dining room table, she made us tuna casserole for dinner.

Tara was excited and proud to be entertaining her friends in her new place. I wanted her to feel good about herself, so I may have poured it on a little thick when I complimented her on the casserole. It was not the best thing I ever put in my mouth, and I shouldn't have eaten so much, but I wanted to prove how much I liked it. That backfired on me because it gave me an uncomfortable bloated stomach and I became a wet blanket on the evening. I was tired and not feeling well, so I just wanted to go home. I still feel awful about being the cause of that lost evening of epic drinking. That was the last time I ever saw Tara.

My girlfriend and I moved to Kelowna B.C. at the end of November 1998. I had wanted to move to Kelowna since I was a teen spending my summers in the Okanagan. For me, Kelowna is the best place to live in the entire world. I was the Assistant General Manager at the Cheese Cake Cafe in February of 2000. My girlfriend phoned me in hysterics, and she was frantically crying, trying to speak but not saying anything. She finally collected herself long enough to blurt out what had happened.

At first, details were sketchy, all we knew for sure was that she was killed by a fatal blow to the head. The people that found her said she was convulsing in a pool of blood and vomit, Tara died at the hospital. The lack of information drove me to create scenarios in my head, and I would imagine how it must have happened. The cash register was taken, which meant Tara did not open it for him. Knowing Tara, she probably thought it was a joke. Maybe Tara laughed at him, and he smashed her head in out of anger. Maybe she shut down in fear; she couldn't move, as he screamed at her to open the cash register, and crushed her skull out of frustration. Those made up scenarios were plausible, it was much later when we found out what actually happened just before midnight on February 17, 2000. While it is slow Tara keeps busy with the cleaning duties and believes she is all alone; she doesn't notice that a man has slipped into the sandwich shop. The man waits for his opportunity, creeps up behind her and with a sledgehammer, caves her skull in. He needs money for crack, and exchanges Tara's life for the 200 dollars he gets from the till. The 32-year-old man gets his drugs that night, but later receives a life sentence with no parole for 18 years, for the second-degree murder of Tara, she was only 25 years old.

My girlfriend left for Calgary a few days after hearing the news. She went to her funeral. She joined the protests that helped change legislation regarding employees working late by themselves. I couldn't go, I had to work, being alone gave me a lot of time to contemplate everything. I would think what a terrible person that crackhead asshole was, his presence in this world has left pain and sorrow. Rocked to my core, I began to reflect on myself, and asked myself what kind of person am I. I don't want to be the villain in another person's story, or my existence affect the planet negatively. I weighed the positive and negative influences I had as I watched my truck warm-up. Then there was the realization that the particular carbon monoxide spewing from my truck wouldn't exist if I weren't here. It was in that moment that I decided I needed to be responsible for myself, and set forth my commitment to have a positive effect in this world.

I loved my truck, probably more than a person should have for something that is not alive. Then again, once you turn the key, she comes alive. She was a red Ford 150XLT Lariat, with dual tanks, extended box, and a super cab. I spent 100s of hours with her, we drove across Canada together, and she would move anything I asked her. I would clean, polish, and change the oil not because I had too, but because I wanted to.

When it was time for new tires or windshield wipers, it was nothing but the best. She had running boards, so stepping into her was slick. The Captain's chair was amazing, how it conformed to my body. The fold-down armrests combined perfectly with the tilt steering, and with the cruise control located at my fingertips, it made driving through Saskatchewan a breeze. She started like a dream, first try every time even in extreme cold, and she idled so smooth it was like she wasn't running. I double started her a couple of times because I didn't think she was running. I would always forget to turn down the stereo before I turned her on. I would often accidentally startle passengers with an insane volume blast of Metallica. I also love music, and my truck had a kick-ass sound system. Full, rich sound that I would crank and sing to at the top of my lungs. She was a climate-controlled rock concert on wheels, inside that world, there was an energy that would get my adrenaline flowing, my heart accelerating.

Not using my truck proved to be a challenge. I had decided to try to walk to the store sometimes, the grocery store was a 15-minute walk from my house. With my truck, I could get there and park in five minutes. When it was raining, I would drive, if it were hot out, I would drive. Even if it was just perfect outside, I would be half-way there in my truck before I realized I was supposed to be walking. It's an automatic routine to jump in and motor to where ever you need to go. She was a temptress, and I knew I couldn't resist her. I had to let her go if I was to fulfill my resolve. I needed to make being alive not result in hurting the planet, and make the carbon monoxide from my truck my responsibility.

It was April 30, 2000, and I took my baby to a local used car lot. I didn't want to go through a private sale and have people test-driving her, and I thought it would be easier if I sold her quickly. I didn't get much for her, a whole lot less than what she was worth to me. It was overcast that morning but not raining, it had rained a couple of hours before, and the streets were still wet. The walk home from the used car lot felt excruciatingly long. I gave up a trusted and reliable friend and replaced it with wet shoes and cold feet.

The following year was a learning process. It took 50 minutes to walk to Orchard Park Mall from my house. I eventually realized there were not enough hours in the day where I could spend two hours picking something up at the mall; walking didn't work for me. Besides the time factor, my feet were sore, and carrying heavy shopping bags at your side for extended amounts of time results in a painful achiness on your shoulders.

My girlfriend did not support my decision to sell our transportation. I was an idiot to think that eliminating the carbon monoxide from my truck would make any difference at all. Of course, she was right; my carbon monoxide is a mere puff in the hundreds of million vehicles in North America. I needed to clean my conscious; if the world becomes inhabitable due to human pollution, I wasn't part of it. She was resentful that I wouldn't be able to drive her around anymore, taxi was her mode of transportation now. Walking turned out not to be feasible for me, so I started to take cabs as well. I found out quite quickly that taking a taxi every time I need to go somewhere can grow quite costly. I am also still polluting, only now it is the cab burning fossil fuel.

A year passed since the separation of my beloved, I was still dreaming of her in my dreams. The longing to touch her, hoping that somehow, we would be reunited. We used to be inseparable, always so supportive of each other, we were soulmates. I am of course referring to my truck; my girlfriend stuck around for a little longer.

I did not own a bike, but I knew how to ride one, I loved to ride as a kid. I was six when my dad gave me my first two-wheeler. There were training wheels on it, but my dad took them off before giving it to me; he didn't believe in them. He would teach me how to ride the bike when he got time. In the back yard was a poplar tree, I could lean my bike against it and climb on to the seat. Once there, I could imagine riding my bike like a motorcycle, complete with sound effects. Soon, I was bored with pretending; I wanted to ride. I place my foot on the top pedal, put all my weight on it, and push down. I sluggishly moved forward about two feet, and I fall over. I'm not hurt;

the lawn is thick and plush. I do it again and again until I keep my balance long enough to push down on the other pedal. I'm excited; pretty soon, I'm up to three pushes. I was so impressed with myself that I dropped my bike to run into the house to let my mom know I am riding my bike for real. After a slight acknowledgment from my mom, I was back at it.

Our gravel driveway ran alongside our house, so I propped my bike up against the house. The problem with that is I do not yet possess the ability to turn. A few minutes later and I'm back inside crying because I'm bleeding from my elbow when I scraped it against the rough plaster on the house. Blood oozed out of the bits of gravel embedded in my knee that I got from falling over on the driveway. After receiving medical attention from my mom, I returned to the forgiveness of the Poplar tree and the lawn. That evening my dad parked the car in the driveway, so I lean my bike against it and am able to ride straight up the driveway. It didn't take long until I was pedaling as fast as I could, slamming on the brakes and skidding on the gravel.

Larry's bike shop was only a few blocks away from my house, that's where I bought a black Supercycle. They wanted $110; I offered $90, we settled on $100. I rode it home, and I knew I had found my transportation. It was a Canadian Tire bike, heavy with clumsy gears, but it got me to where I needed to go in a fraction of the time it took to walk. The problem with grocery bags on your handlebars is that they sway side to side and will eventually swing into your spokes. The bag rips, and there is a can of corn rolling down the street.

The backpack is a game-changer and is essential to using a bike as transportation. Backpacks that zip, would split from excessive loads, the style with the drawstring and flap cover is a superior design for carrying heavy loads. Some stores will harass me because of my backpack. They will approach me and inform me that I must leave it behind the counter at customer service. They say that it is company policy; they are enforcing theft prevention protocol. Most of the time, I comply, sometimes I would leave and go to another store. However, I get irritated with these confrontations, by accosting me in the middle of the store, they are telling me and everyone within earshot, that they don't trust me not to steal. I have never taken anything from these stores; In fact, I spent 1000s of dollars at the one store back when I had my truck. Now, for no reason other than my backpack, I am treated like a criminal. At the mall, I would lock up my bag in the lockers so I could move freely from store to store. I avoided certain stores if shopping there meant that my character would come into question. I do not support companies that disrespect me for being green; Walmart and Superstore remain the only businesses that have never asked me to remove my backpack.

There are screws for a water bottle cage on every bike because riding makes your mouth very dry, but I have issues with this thirst-quenching method. A bottle will go flying with a sudden stop, tight turn, or jumping a curb. I found drinking and biking do not mix, not just water but alcohol too. This discovery was made one night after a New Year's Eve party. I fell over on my bike every six feet, and after falling 20 times, I walked the rest of the way home. To take a drink from a water bottle, you have to steer with one hand and hold it with the other and tilt your head back. Lack of control combined with your eyes leaving the road is a recipe for disaster. If a car door opens up into the bike lane and you're taking a drink, you will die.

The water gets warm and tastes like plastic, cleaning and refilling takes time. Not to mention that after all that, water hydrates but doesn't work for dry mouth on a bike. A sip of water will buy about 30 seconds before a mouth becomes a desert again. Chewing gum, turned out to be the best solution, but mint-flavor upsets my stomach. Cinnamon sugar-free gum is the only gum for me; it freshens my breath as well as it keeps my mouth from drying out. The craziest thing happens when riding and chewing for a long time; after an hour or two, it starts to break apart and dissolve. Epiphany, the old tale that you shouldn't swallow gum because it takes a long time to digest is false.

The only thing I am missing now is a rock concert on wheels. Every year the advancement of electronics brings out a new system and changes the way I listen music. My first was an Iriver MP3 player; it had 512mb of space. Earbuds were a frustrating problem, riding a bike in the city requires a lot of shoulder checks; the turning of my head makes the earbuds fall out. Steering with one hand is okay if you are going straight. Turning, stopping, or traveling through an intersection requires both on the handlebars. I would be listening to my favorite tunes, and the earbuds would continually fall out, and having to reinsert them so repeatedly is annoying. Then, one of the sides will crackle or cut in and out, or stop working altogether, and it's time to replace. I tried the earphones that wrap around the ear, a few pulls on the wire, and they are finished. Sony introduced a Walkman with a two GB MP3 player built into the earpiece. I had wanted a product like this for years, so I was excited to see them finally on the market. They were so perfect; no wires were hanging from my head, and it would never fall from my ears. Unfortunately, the early models had poor battery performance and didn't make it through the winter. The second one I bought didn't make it through winter either, and ultimately, I decided earbuds are too dangerous. I use the speaker on my phone now; it has 32GB of space and has a very impressive sound.

The days immediately following Tara's murder were filled with utter sadness. Friends don't usually get murdered; it left me traumatized, and with an awful numbness. Tragic events can trigger a more philosophical outlook and change the road you're on. Not only has this event changed my path, but without a doubt, it altered how I got there. I have ridden my bike every day for the last 20 years; I did my best not to burn any fossil fuel.

Chapter Two
Spring

The air is different in the spring, unlike any other time of the year. The last of the snow is in the shade for most of the day, and I am on the lookout for the first Robin of the year. Seeing a Robin means spring has arrived, a welcoming sight after months of a bitter winter. Blades of green grass are sprouting up everywhere; there are pussy-willows and cherry blossoms in the trees. Rejuvenated by the air, the sun shining warmly on my face, and inspired by the signs of life, the rides to work and back are more enjoyable each day.

The world goes by much slower on a bike, which allows for the appreciation of the little things. There is a lot of action in the spring if you are a bird lover like me. Osprey Park is a baseball field and a soccer field with an Osprey nest that sits on a pole high above the world. A perfect location for a couple of love birds to call their summer home.

The bike path to work runs alongside the park; as I get closer, my eyes scan the skyline for signs of their return. I am anxious, it is nearing the end of April, the Ospreys are usually back by now. Maybe during their migration, they were shot and killed; I tried not to think the worst. Then one day, they are majestically soaring in the air, high in the sky. Seeing them again gave me a calmness and a feeling that everything is right in the world. Each year I watch them raise a baby Osprey, but not this year. There will be no youngster perched on the edge of the nest, spreading his wings for a test flap. Most years, the female doesn't fly much; she stays home while he hunts. This year they are both flying around, although I think he is still bringing her food. She stays in the nest while he isn't around, maybe he's at the lake picking up fresh fish for dinner. I rode that route for eight years, and they had a single offspring every year, but that one. Riding by only took a minute, but day after day, the minutes add up. There and back, I spent two minutes a day checking in on them. I am grateful for the accumulated 40 hours in one-minute intervals in which I got to admire those impressive predators.

Along that same trail was a ditch that was frequented by many critters. On my way by, I would say hi to my friends the ducks. The ducks are locals and stay for the winter, they like this patch of water because it doesn't freeze often. They are nervous about me the first few times I ride by; most fly away. Some stay; they swim around looking cute, always keeping one eye on me. It isn't long before they grow accustomed to me riding by and stop flying away. Only blue-green male Mallards are left after a few weeks of spring; the females are away nesting, and the males stay to feed.

Blue Herons are beautiful giant birds, it is always cool to see one; every once in a while, one would be standing in the bulrushes. When this happened, I would stop and watch him until I was spotted, then he would calmly stretch his massive wings wide before stroking the air and lifting to the sky. He flies up and away from me, does a U-turn and flies overhead to another marshy area with a little more privacy. Also, in that patch of water lived a Muskrat, most days I can see where he is from the water rippling as he swims under the surface. One time I saw him on the bank of the ditch, he was a small weasel-like animal that loves water, from what I can remember, it was a Muskrat. Once while hunting with my dad, he shot a duck that fell into the water, and a Muskrat seized the opportunity to grab a quick lunch. Honestly, that is my only frame of reference to determine it was a Muskrat.

Spring brings new love, my new girlfriend and I moved in together. As a gesture of cuteness, I gave her two baby Muscovy Ducks for our big fenced backyard. I read Muscovy Ducks ate a lot of insects, and my girlfriend was terrified of bugs, especially spiders. They were named Chuck and Daisy; they became family. They did eat a ton of bugs, and when they are not eating, they are humping. The male chases the female and pins her down to the ground. Then he stands on her, and sometimes in his maneuvering, he stands on her head. She doesn't seem to mind the roughness, but it's kind of looks like duck rape to me. That's Mother Nature, and pretty soon, there were babies; adorable, cuddly ducklings that fit in the palm of my hand and melted my heart. They stayed inside for the first two weeks; however, ducks are perpetual crappers. At first, there were tiny little droppings that were hardly noticeable, but the chicks grew, and their turds were getting bigger and more frequent. I was anxious to introduce them to their permanent home, the outside. Their food and water station were in a gazebo so that the duck food would stay dry when it rained. Two kid-sized pools were sitting in thick grass, inviting all to splash around. The surrounding five-foot fence kept them from getting out and provided security from any predators getting in; it was a duck paradise.

I didn't know it at the time, but someone was watching me. A Crow swooped down and snatched one of my baby ducks the moment I went inside. In the back corner of the yard was a cherry tree with a doghouse under it. My neighbor was retired and often watched the ducks from her window. She said the Crow took the baby to the roof of the doghouse. A duckling makes an instinctively non-stop cute chirping sounds so that the mother always knows where her babies are. I imagine the baby chick was frantically calling for its mother as it was eaten alive. I didn't see it happen; I can see that the incident shook my neighbor as she recounts what she had witnessed. Piece after piece, the crow takes another bite of its victim. The baby is still alive and is crying for its mother, being eaten one morsel at a time. I wonder how long the chick suffered before the fatal strike that brings the mercy of death.

I love birds; they are a beautiful compliment to the world around us. They swoop, glide, flap, chirp, sing, and they make babies. No one needs to tell me Crows kill other birds, I know from experience. They are scavengers, protected by the Migratory Bird Treaty Act created over 100 years ago; it is illegal to kill a crow in Canada. My dad shot a Crow once; it was the first dead animal I ever saw; I was five. I shot a Crow once; it came into my yard and murdered one of my babies. I own a 12-gauge shotgun, but live within city limits, fueled by anger, I had thoughts that would most likely get me in trouble. I also have a collection of air guns; they are way cheaper on ammo if all your doing is target practice. One of those air guns stood out above all the rest for distance, accuracy, and being whisper-quiet. With this gun, I could knock the eraser of a pencil at 30 feet. Perched high in the Cherry tree, the Crow has returned and is scanning the yard for another snack. The chicks are back inside until they get bigger.

I am in a vengeful mood, one hand on my gun, the other slowly and quietly slides open the window. I had deliberately removed the screen prior, providing a clear shot of the enemy. As a boy, my cousin and

I hunted birds and squirrels in the forest near his house. We were killing machines armed with high compression air rifles; we were a menace to all small animals. I have impeccable aim from all the years of practice, so I probably could have targeted that Crow's head and made the shot, however aiming for the body has a higher percentage of a kill. There was a slight breeze, and the branches were swaying just a little. I was aiming for the heart; a bird will fall like a rock if you shoot them through the heart. At this distance, it will be a through and through.

As a curious youth, I often examined a kill for an entry wound and an exit wound. Not to be morbid, my dad told me never let an animal suffer, and I wanted to know where to shoot that would result in the quickest death. I lock on my target; I hear my dad's voice in my head say don't pull the trigger, breathe out, and squeeze it. There is a distinct sound that hitting center mass makes and I just heard it. I made good contact but missed the heart; still, it was only a matter of time before it would succumb to that type of injury. Shocked and not sure of what has happened, the crow tries to collect itself, and after several attempts, it takes flight never to return.

I didn't celebrate my vengeful kill for the life of a loved one, it didn't bring any satisfaction. Instead, I find myself having empathy for the crow; I feel shame and never tell another soul what I had done. I wanted to feel justified, an eye for an eye justice; I just didn't. Feeling awful about my actions didn't change the fact that I now hate Crows. Every time I see one, it reminds me of that helpless innocent fluffy sweet little guy screaming, as pieces of flesh are torn from its body until finally, a last breath.

If they are attacking prey in my back yard, then they are most definitely doing that in the wild to all the other birds. They do not just scavenge; they are also highly intelligent and cunning predator that will take a new life given the opportunity. By protecting the Crows, the government has endangered the other birds. Crows are annoyingly loud when you are trying to sleep in, and are always digging through the garbage, making a mess on the street. Farmers have found them to be a nuisance and would rather they not be around. There needs to be a culling of Crows, the numbers are over 30 million and rising.

Wetland loss due to the expansion of man has long thought to be the culprit when discussing bird extinction, but this explanation doesn't fall under the umbrella of reason for me. My Ducks build nests that I promptly remove them, as we have no room for more ducks. The next day she has constructed another nest at a different location. I see empty marshy areas all the time; these should be overcrowded with birds if the problem is a shortage of wetland. I can see it with my own two eyes; there are a lot fewer birds than there used to be. I suggest that the over 30 million crows may have eaten some of those birds' babies. A murder of Crows moves place to place, devouring the young of the defenseless.

One of those black demons lures the mother from her nest, then its partner in crime snatches her baby and flies off. The survival of a variety of birds could be dependent on the removal of Crows from the protection list. There is a staggering three billion fewer birds in North America than there was 50 years ago; I would consider the Bird Migration act of 1918 an extremely ineffective attempt to protect our precious bird population.

Poison is another contributor to the bird genocide and possibly the cause of the desperate bee situation. Enormous amounts of poison, continuously for decades, floods the air thanks to humankind's ingenuity. That is not to mention the countless animal lives lost to oil spills around the world. What a sad world we live in when there are no birds to swoop, glide, flap, chirp, sing, and have babies.

Rain in spring is much appreciated as it washes away winters' dirty secrets once hidden under the snow, the mysterious bits of black and debris that line the bike paths. Winter is over, and I couldn't be happier about it, the novelty had long worn off. The smell of freshly cut lawn after it rains ranks as one of my top five aroma experiences. I use an old-school lawnmower, the kind with gears and rotating blades, powered by me. I had read that a gas lawn mower is responsible for 80 lbs. of emissions a year. Of course, with my luck, I received this information right after I bought a brand new Lawnboy, which sat there mocking me until the day someone stole it.

Pushing a manual mower is a little bit of a workout, and it also takes longer because I have to do two passes then rake. I use a file to sharpen the blades razor-sharp and mow once a week; the longer the grass the harder to cut. Sunday is the day I do yard work, and if I'm lucky, I am done everything right before it rains. One of the best of the little things, is to watch nature feed the immaculate piece of art you have just groomed. Most of the time in Kelowna it rains for about 20 minutes and stops. Then the sun comes out, and blades of green glisten under a bright new rainbow. When the last drops of miracle juice fall from the sky, and you watch the final drip from a thirsty leaf, that's when you can smell it. It's like your snuggling up to mother nature herself, so crisp and fresh. Incredibly intoxicating, I can't get enough, and breath in the transcendent air to the point of hyperventilation, sometimes the little things can be the sweetest. The other aroma experiences are, the first few minutes when you get to the lake, the smell after slicing a cucumber, bread baking, and the waterfalls at Johnston's canyon in Banff.

I look out into the pouring rain, it's time to go to work, and I struggle with the realization that for the next 45 minutes I am going to get drenched. Sometimes if you wait 20 minutes, it will stop. It's been 30, and I have no choice, leave, or be late. I put a raincoat on if it's raining super hard, but it is mostly ineffective; the material holds in the heat, so it feels like a sauna and I am swimming in sweat by the time I get there. I pack dry socks and underwear in a zip-lock, I also have a towel and a change of clothes in a plastic bag inside my backpack, so I will be able to dry off and get out of my wet things when I get there.

I can hear the rain teeming down as I open the garage door, I can't see across the street from the rain. I dive right in; I have to make up for the time I procrastinated and begin my commute. With each push of the pedal, I get further from the warmth of home. The drops echo on my hood, and it reminds me of the sound when in a tent during a rain shower. The spring rain is cold; my fingers are stiff; I tuck them into my hand in efforts to get feeling back. My speed starts to increase; my hands clamp down on the grips; for the next two kilometers, it's all downhill. On a typical day, I let loose and fly down as fast as gravity will take me. Today the dirty road water sprays off the front tire into my face, and halfway down it blinds my left eye. I slow down; in fear dirt makes it into my other eye and I will lose my sight completely.

I like spring showers, but this year, 2018, it is getting ridiculous; there is flooding in the valley; many areas are declared states of emergency, Kelowna is hit hard. Halfway to work, Bulman road is closed, Mill Creek burst its banks and has swallowed the street in front of me. The adjacent field where cows will graze in the summer is a lake. I notice that it is shallow along the center line and carefully navigate down it. Water splashes up at me, but I am not getting any wetter. There is a city worker at the end of the street who is enforcing the closure, he gives me a look as I ride by, I smile. I have maneuvered the flooded road and am continuing on my way. I live on a mountain, and my work is in a raised area of the city, so it's business as usual for me, I am basically unaffected by the flood.

Of all the time I have spent on the road, I rarely get caught in the rain, but when it does happen, it's OK, it's only water. When it happens on my way home, I jump in the shower and go from cold and wet to enveloped by a warm euphoric waterfall that makes my skin tingle with soothing waves of pleasure. It is a remarkable experience and not possible without getting uncomfortably wet first.

Spring is good-bye winter and welcome summer, with a splash of the miracle of life. Unfortunately, if we don't rectify the declining bird populations, the miracle of life may be soon reduced to a trickle. If birds are not swooping, gliding, flapping, chirping, singing, and having babies, then the world is not a better place because we existed, and we are the villains of this story.

Chapter Three
Summer

Sometimes it gets so hot you can fry an egg on the sidewalk; today's high is 42 degrees C, 107.6 degrees F; summer has arrived. The Okanagan summer brings the heat; it delivers hot sunny days with very little precipitation. Rain takes a vacation in July and August; it would be a welcome break from the extreme heat if it would just drop down some moisture. I step out of the air-conditioning into the hellish conditions of the outside; It feels hot as hell. The air feels hot against the skin inside my nose; not only can I smell summer, but I have the sensation of it. Beads of sweat form instantly on my forehead from nothing but the friction of passing air.

I have to remind myself to slow down and pedal with the least amount of exertion; I am not setting any speed records today. There are heat waves on the asphalt ahead, but I am sweating only slightly. As long as my bike is moving forward, air fans over my skin drying the sweat faster than it can flow. If I stop now, even for 30 seconds, sweat will pour out of me like a dam broke. Timing the traffic lights is essential; I slow down on an upcoming red and speed up if it's green. Almost there, it is important that I don't upset the balance of speed to perspiration ratio.

Safeway is across the street from work and is my destination for their superb air-conditioning. Once there, the rush is on to lock my bike and get inside; the sweat is coming. This Safeway is not only a slice of heaven for the coolest air-conditioning but also has a Starbucks inside. I order an iced Frappuccino, and while the barista prepares my beverage; I find a vent to stand under, I have sprung a leak from my skin. The first sips are like drinking a miracle and a few glacier-sized pulls of the sweet magic elixir, and I turned back into a human.

When I was a kid on the school bus, we would use steamy breath on the windows to make condensation. With my finger, I would draw a heart with an arrow through it, or play tic-tac-toe with a friend. When I get brain-freeze, I pretend like I'm breathing on a window three to four times; I basically blow hot air at my brain, and it's gone. It is true, if you drink hot beverages during the day it will lower the body's core temperature, but if already overheated, nothing beats a blended ice drink.

Riding a bike every day means more one on one time with the pesky bugs. Swarms of tiny black flies' hover over the bike paths, patiently waiting for the chance to fly into my eye. I don't see them until it's too late; bombarded by multiple enemy suicide attacks, my sunglasses fail to protect, and the intruder finds its target. I frantically fight back by trying to blink it out; it refuses to give up and dies in my eye. I continue riding, hampered by blurred vision and the discomfort of a mashed-up insect in the corner of my eye. I will need a tissue and a mirror to clean up the aftermath of this unprovoked attack.

I ride hard most of the time; the faster I pedal, the quicker I get there. That results in heavy breathing; sometimes, I am unaware I am breathing through my mouth, and surprise, a giant housefly flies straight in and down my throat. Not cool; I try to spit it out, but it is too far in there; I try coughing it up, and now I'm gagging. Nothing left to do but swallow, I am nauseous and might throw up, I can feel the monstrous flying germ carrier, it's stuck half-way down. Moments before, it was most likely in rotten garbage or sitting on a fresh pile of dog crap, so gross. An experience I can live without repeating; I do my best to avoid eating bugs, and I make it a policy to never ride with my mouth open.

Mosquito bites on the ankle are the worst, with an itchy welt on the elbow, a close second. My backpack protects my back from getting bit, but the back of my shoulders is exposed, and I am penetrated in that juicy location several times a day in the summer dusk. Each day I go down the mountain only to have to go back up. Going down is fast and exciting coming back up is slow and is quite a workout. The main problem with climbing steep inclines in the summer is that if my speed is too slow, the bloodsuckers will get me. My accelerated exhales of carbon dioxide are chiming the dinner bell for any mosquito around to come feast on my sweet blood.

My skin does not react well when wearing repellent and sweating; I get a nasty rash. I think getting bit through sweat might make it itchier; I do my best not to scratch. Some people say to press an x in a mosquito bite with your fingernail, and I will try anything once. I tried that method several times, the itchiness worsens and it takes longer to heal. I have also tried the commercial ammonia products that comes in a stick; people are desperate for relief from the inane itchiness. For me, at least, it made it even more itchy; and calamine lotion is not any better. My mom told me to stop scratching, and as it turns out, it's the most effective way to treat a mosquito bite is to do nothing at all. It is quite difficult to resist the urge to give in, but a whisper of a scratch leads to two, and soon it looks like you are trying to start a fire on your arm. Mind over matter; I force my fingers to resist the temptation because I know if I am successful, it is usually gone by the next day.

At the end of my street, there are several undeveloped lots in a row, overgrown weeds, and generally not kept. On this particular day, someone, probably the city, mowed the entire area; the clean-up improved the look of the field. I passed by wondering if they were about to start building in this location. Then it hit me, the largest bee I have ever seen, the size of a gumball, right in the throat. This bee more than likely had her home destroyed from the lot clean-up and is exceptionally agitated; I am an innocent victim in the wrong place at the wrong time. When it hit, it hit hard; I could feel the impact of its abnormally large body smash into me, then off the charts level of pain in my neck. The queen bee doesn't leave behind a stinger; she delivers only intense pain that lasted for about 40 minutes. That is followed by a dull throbbing and swelling, I approximate that it is 20 times worse that of a mosquito bite, and lasts a couple of weeks.

It's summertime, and I am enjoying the evening weather, dressed in shorts and a t-shirt, the air is still warm from the day as it passes over my skin. I hit a green light and cruise through the intersection only to be greeted by an aggressive wasp who rams me in the chest and does the dance of pain. Initially, it feels like an electric shock as he moves violently, penetrating my shirt and into my flesh. Much like the bee sting, it also delivers 40 minutes of agony, ten on the pain scale. This Yellow Jacket's venom makes my chest muscle stiff and achy. There is also swelling and bruising; the skin around the bite is black and blue, which took three weeks to heal. I was assaulted once again, maybe by the same wasp, it was at the same intersection a month later. I was ready this time, and I managed to flick him off quick with the back of my hand the moment he touched my neck. Not fast enough though, in that brief millisecond, he managed to get me, not as bad as the previous sting, painful but with less swelling. I am not sure if it was the same angry wasp, and it had a vendetta against me, or it was an entirely different wasp, and I am just an irresistible target. Getting stung is not a regular occurrence being that these are the only times in 20 years that it's happened to me.

The sun shines a weak pink-orange hue as it struggles to break through the thick smoke and ash. There are fires all around us; visibility is poor, the sun is merely a small circle suspended in the sky. August without smoke is rare in the past 20 years, the last two have set records for the most fires and the most damage. People are walking around with surgical masks on, and are having difficulty breathing. I cannot wear a mask because the condensation build-up and makes it too hard to breathe through. I take in air carefully through my nose, hoping I don't snort any of the falling chunks of ash.

The summer of 2018 is host to the most devastating fire season of all-time in B.C, with 2117 fires and 1,354,284 hectares lost. The year before boasts the previous historical record, the fire seasons are getting worse. Airports are canceling flights due to poor visibility from the dense smoke and ash. The people not evacuated are put on alert, meaning they have to be ready to leave at a moment's notice. All the hotels are full; emergency shelters are set up for the evacuees.

Billowing black smoke rises from the direction of my house as I begin my final ascent. I am worried and hoping that it is not my house; I lost my first house in Kelowna when a fire started due to an over-heated air-conditioner. That is something I don't want to go through again; I check the skyline to see if it still looks like it's coming from my house. The closer I get, the more I realize that the smoke is not coming from my house. The relief is short-lived; the cloud of thick black smoke is now a massive black monster and is uncomfortably close. The first thing I do once in the door, check online for any information. My area is under evacuation alert, and are to wait for further instructions. Crews have responded and are aggressively attacking it as there are many houses threatened. I place a few items that I can't live without by the door, the last report before bed says the fire is under control.

The city firefighters responded first, followed by water bombers and forest firefighters. The next morning only puffs of white smoke rise from the ground, thanks to our protectors who so expertly managed and extinguished the beast of death. There are two houses that don't escape the devil's dance and have been consumed by it. The cause of this tragedy is determined to be arson, a person witnessed someone lighting dry grass at the bottom of the hill.

It is easier to start a fire than ever thanks to climate change, forest fires rage not only here, but also in California, Spain, Greece, Australia, Brazil, and is a worldwide concern. Weather is becoming more extreme with each year; I'm just saying, there was no thunder snow when I was growing up. Hurricanes and floods, droughts, and fires are increasing in frequency and ferocity. Drought has gripped the Okanagan summer; it's been two months since we felt a drop of rain.

It feels like the end of days; the sun choked out of the sky, the world is on fire, and its eerily quiet outside, people are staying at home. It would be easy to see how life would cease to exist if not for the sun; the growing season is already hindered by the lack of sunlight. I pedal along with minimal side effects from the smoke; I have healthy strong lungs, and I travel at near usual speed. Nightfall comes earlier than most; darkness fills the sky by the time I get to the bottom of Quail Ridge, my daily climb. In the streetlights, the ash falls like huge flakes of snow; I start breathing heavier the further up the mountain I get. I am half-way, and out of breath, my lungs can't take anymore, and I have to start walking my bike.

When I get home, I go to the bathroom to wash my face. I look in the mirror, and looking back at me is a soldier right out of battle. My skin is covered in gray-black ash, broken up with lines from the sweat that had dripped down my face; I am going to need a shower. My lungs raw from the smoke and ash; I yearn for clear skies.

In my mind, I picture the forest wildlife running frantically to escape the deathly destruction of a wall of flames only to succumb to suffocating black smoke. They would be confused and panicked on which way to go, smoke in every direction compounded by symptoms from lack of oxygen; the bear with her cub cannot escape the uncaring clutches of the fire. Fire is insatiable and rips through the forest at six kilometers per hour, faster if it is traveling uphill. While a deer is much faster, the flames will win with stamina, relentless and unstoppable power that ends all life in its path.

It's my birthday today; I must be getting old as it seems the smoke from the candles on my cake has blocked out the sun. I'm taking the long way home because I did not see a Magpie during my morning ride to work. A random stranger once told me that it is good luck if you see a Magpie on your birthday. Since then, I watch for them, not only on my birthday but every day, I feel better when I see one. My window of opportunity is closing; I become fearful that due to the smoke, I will miss out on this year's good luck bird. I can't afford to miss out on any good luck that the universe might have up for grabs. There is a forgotten pile of old scrap wood; tall weeds are growing through, and around it, it sits on gravel at the long-abandoned McCurdy train yard. That is where my eyes welcomed in two magpies, dancing and playing. The complementary sharpness of the white on black, along with a squeaky chirp, sleek body, and a long tail, make the Magpie, one of my favorite birds. I rode by them, relieved, grateful, and thankful for their presence. They are the sight of optimism: finally, this will be my lucky year.

Maybe it is a sign of the apocalypse when one minute we are drowning in water, the next we are burning in fire. The increase of extreme weather is palpable; I can see it, and feel it; the warning signs of a changing environment. Sound the alarms, we are under attack, this is not a drill, if you open your eyes, you will see science is right; we don't have much time left, and perhaps we are in the autumn of our species.

Chapter Four
Autumn

The best weather for biking is in early fall, September and October are my favorite months for riding. The sky is clear; the air is crisp as Geese fly overhead in an arrow formation, seemingly pointing out the direction they are going. The leaves turn from green to orange-brown, and the temperature drops; I can feel the tingle in my ear lobes, fingers, and toes. It's time to dig out the winter clothes, say good-bye to t-shirts and shorts, welcome gloves, winter jacket, and track pants. I am able to ride harder, now that the temperature has cooled. The chilly nights and the smell of burning wood in fireplaces is an ominous sign; winter is coming.

Daylight savings time has no benefit in current times, yet twice a year, we deal with it anyway. Most of my devices set the on their own without any prompting; the clock on the stove is going to be an hour fast for the next six months. It must be easier to make new laws than to retire the outdated ones, as it is still illegal to ride your horse on Bernard Avenue without a diaper, even though it is illegal to ride your horse downtown. The government could avoid redundancies if they had a spring cleaning once a year to retire laws that are ineffective or not applicable anymore.

The darkness comes earlier and earlier each night, and it is time for me to shine; I have two red lights on both sides of my backpack and a very bright headlight. I click them on, I leave work, and I am on my way home. It is 9:30 on a Thursday; the air is calm; the night is dark as molasses. I am not in a hurry, but I am making good time, there is barely any traffic; it's a quick ride to the trail at Osprey Park. Now I start riding faster, it's a straight away, and I am getting closer to home. The trail runs along railway tracks left behind from a bygone era, trains are not coming into Kelowna anymore; between the path and the tracks is a chain-link fence running the length of the trail. Suddenly I see him, a big beautiful male whitetail deer with big impressive antlers, I surprise him with my stealthy approach, my bike doesn't make any noise, so I am mere feet away before he notices me. Startled, he starts running, not away from me, but alongside me, I pedal a little harder to keep pace. He pounds the ground with his hooves, his muscles ripple in his powerful shoulders. His heavy hot breath is steaming clouds of smoke out of his nose that disappear in the night. He did not turn off like I expected him to do, he is in a full gallop; I am almost at my top speed, then time stopped, and we shared a moment of connection. His large glassy black eye continues to be locked on me, mystically peering into my soul until the end of the trail, where we parted ways.

Autumn in Canada allows you to watch the world die right in front of your eyes; the leaves are colorful just before they crumble into dust. People stop living outside and entomb themselves in their homes. Fireplaces burn wood until there is nothing left but ash. Fruit is devoured right off the tree, the harvest is in, and the crops are lifeless. Soon a blanket of snow will hide the faltering earth and I will long for summer days.

Chapter Five
Winter

A fluffy snowflake hangs in the air before it slowly falls to its death as it melts on the sidewalk, it's the first snowfall. I call it cosmetic snow; it looks pretty, and there is no need to shovel. It's colder for the second snowfall; small flecks tickle my upper lip, nose, and cheeks; it smothers the world of color; for the next three months, it's black and white. The north wind blows; the last two leaves on the tree finally release their waning grip and race to the ground, winter has come. I dig out a large cardboard box of winter clothes out of the closet, I pull out a pair of full-length long-johns and hope that I won't need these this year. I dress according to the temperature; the long-johns are necessary once the mercury dips below minus 20 degrees Celsius. When it hits 25 below zero, the world is entirely different; it's an inhabitable deep freeze.

It is 5:30 am, time to leave the toasty comfort of home and brave the elements, the thermometer says minus 25, at least it's not minus 50. I got to know what minus 50 degrees Celsius feels like working a job in Tisdale, Saskatchewan, and it's all kinds of messed up. I am in Kelowna, and so far, minus 25 is the coldest I have ridden in, today is one of those days when I have to check my resolve. At times like this, I like to remember some inspirational, motivating quotes from my dad. He would say something like aah poor muffin or suck it up princess, or the classic, poor baby; what he meant was, when times get tough, then it is time to toughen up. People tell me how impossible it is, and I respond with a shoulder shrug, smile and jokingly say something to the effect of not if you're a real man.

I don't start getting dressed until just before I am stepping out into the bone-chilling cold. Long-johns first, a one-piece holds in heat better than separate top and bottom, socks are next because they keep the long underwear from sliding up my leg. Sport socks covered by wool socks, then sweatpants, t-shirt, long-sleeved shirt, flannel, hoodie. I put on my lined track pants before I place my feet in plastic bags and slide on my winter boots; without the plastic bags, my feet will sweat into my boot liner, then freeze, and my feet are encased in ice. My winter coat is wind and waterproof; I put on a balaclava and scarf, the hood over my head, and thick mitts.

It is not snowing, but no one told two small stray flakes falling from the dark sky into the glow of the streetlight across from my house. The world is still asleep; I am all alone just how I like it, then a car drives by and leaves a cloud of smoke behind it; at this temperature, the carbon monoxide takes longer to mix with the frigid non-receptive air. I ride through it, and it coats the inside of my mouth, I hold my breath until I get to some air that is not poisoned. The taste lingers, I am breathing through my tongue, a technique I use to heat the air a little before it gets to my lungs. It is done by blocking the opening of my mouth with my tongue and letting small amounts of air pass through. This trick protects my lungs from the extreme cold that will make them raw and increase my chances of getting sick.

Three inches of ice covers the road, and I am distracted from the cold by frustration with the city's inadequate snow removal; compared to other cities I have lived in, my current city is grossly incompetent. I ride over some rough ice, and it makes loud cracking as the brittle ice breaks loudly under my tire. When there are no cars, I ride in the middle of the street, the tiny glimpses of asphalt peak through the ice where vehicles have worn it down. I can see the headlights of a vehicle approaching, so I pull over to the side, and the ice gets the best of me, and down I go. My heart races, I am startled by how fast I end up on my side, I have slipped countless times but fell only about a dozen times in all my years' cycling. Today the ice is a polished glassy slick surface, luckily, I have several pounds of clothes on, and I barely feel a thing, I get up quickly and walk my bike to the side and wait for the car to pass. I don't want to fall again; I check my balance and look for strips of shallow snow that hasn't transformed into ice from being driven on or walked on.

I am focusing on keeping my center line perfectly perpendicular to the ground and smooth clean pedaling; any jerking movements will upset the perfect balance I have negotiated with gravity. I have started sweating under my clothes now, ten minutes in on a journey that will take an hour and a half. My face struggles with the cold, and my rising body temperature, a drop of sweat drips passed my left eye. Jack Frost is chomping down on my fingers, and I implement pain management, on a scale from one to ten, the pain is a seven. I reassure myself that the pain is only temporary, and only lasts until I am inside and warmed-up.

Half-way there, I stop at the start of the university bike trail and stare down at the sloped skating rink in front of me. The highway plow has covered the path with basketball-sized chunks of ice. It looks like an avalanche happened here as I negotiate through the ice-field, but it's too slippery, and my bike goes down, I am ready this time and leave my bike to fall while I stand and slide on my feet. A technique I developed over the years, biking in the winter, I don't go down with the bike if I can help it. Biking in winter is like skiing in many ways; one way is, if you lose control, keep your balance, and refuse to wipe-out; the only way to get injured is if you hit the ground. I decide to walk the rest of the way down the minefield, even walking is hard, I slip several times, but I have quick reactions and well-developed balance; I don't fall.

At this point, I am longing for the long days of summer; I would welcome a few mosquito bites. The cold is tickling my feet, the pain in my toes is about a five on the pain scale, and getting worse. My eyelashes are coated with ice as I turn the corner to find they didn't plow Ackland road; there is no other option at this point but to keep moving forward. I stand on my pedal, forcing it down, moving forward is requiring maximum effort and progress is painfully slow. I slip on the ice buried under the two feet of snow, it happens ultra-quick, and I am laying in the road, I stand quickly and slip and fall, the ice under the snow is as slick as could be. I need a break from pedaling and walk my bike until I get to a parking lot; they are usually plowed early for employees and customers. I ride till the end of the parking lot then return to walking; the road is not ridable; ride where it's cleared and walk in any snow over 12 inches. Getting to work is taking longer than usual, this street is a nightmare, good thing I left early; dawn is breaking. I finally reach the end of the road just in time to meet-up with a snowplow about to plow the street that I had struggled with for the last 30 minutes. Once I get to Rutland road, it is cleared, but not the bike lanes; they are used to store snow until the spring. The sidewalks are not an option because the city doesn't enforce the sidewalk clearing bylaw, and maybe one in ten shoveled. To add an extra element of danger, I have no choice but to ride on the road. I watch for vehicles, and every time one is coming, I stop and pull my bike onto the snowbank on the side of the road and wait until it passes then continue on my way. The worst is the thick gray snow that has accumulated in the intersections, and it grabs hold of my front tire. The only thing I can do is hold my steering straight and tight until I come to a stop, get off and walk.

I get to work, and I am swimming in sweat, my toes are ice cubes, a ten on the pain scale. I go to the bathroom and take everything off, everything I am wearing is sopping wet. I hold my toes in efforts to warm them and get some blood flowing, and my hand gets too cold from my toes, I switch and blow hot air into my hand. It is a weird feeling to be sweating and freezing at the same time.

It's Christmas eve, and everyone who wished for snow for Christmas got their wish. It is a blizzard, I need a last-minute gift, and the store is 25 minutes one-way. The flakes have turned to icy missiles that feel like they are penetrating the flesh on my face. It was barely snowing when I left; the storm has moved in quickly; the wind is blowing so hard I am barely moving forward. The white stuff is accumulating rapidly, making progress even more challenging, I squint my eyes from the snow, the flakes turn to pellets and is temporally blinding and cold when they hit me in the eyeball. Eventually, I always get there, a thick layer of snow has encased me by the time I arrive at the store, but I shake it off. I do my shopping and set my sights on the warmness of home.

Winter weather is usually the worst the last half of December until the middle of February, two months that make me appreciate warm sunny days. Some days are better than other days; some years are also better than others. I enjoy the good ones, endure the bad ones, and adapt to any obstruction in my way.

Chapter Six
Near-Death

The icy rain is coming down in a heavy drizzle in the darkness; the ride home looks less than appealing tonight. I can feel every drop hit my hair and drip onto my scalp, immediately I am cold and wet, and I have another hour till I get into a hot shower. I have been down this road before, hundreds of times, it is my regular route that starts on Rutland road. I always ride as far to the right as possible, and at the apple orchard there is a broader shoulder, so I move further to the right, doubling the space from the traffic.

The contact is jarring and shocking; I didn't see it coming, the white minivan first hit my left elbow then my handlebars, which tore my hand from the grip. It left a significant dent in the sliding side door; I am in shock and yell loud enough that I know the driver heard me. I know I was heard because the van immediately swerved back onto the road. My arm is painfully numb, and I wonder if it tore off. The hit sped me up and knocked me off course, and I am heading for a wire fence when somehow, I regained my balance and engaged my back brake slowing me down enough to avoid serious injury. I come to a stop and reach over and am relieved to feel my left arm is still there. I am lit up with three very bright lights and am riding eight feet from traffic, so maybe he or she is impaired, and that's why the minivan is speeding away. I tried to get my phone to take a picture, but it only took seconds for the vans taillights to fade into the night. My arm isn't right, and I am in some severe pain from my elbow to my tingly numb fingers. I can't steer with my left hand, but I rest my wrist on the grip and continue at a slow pace. I am happy there is no damage to my bike; the damage to my arm feels like it might have a break. My arm heals in six weeks; unlike the scars on my psyche, the paranoia of getting hit again remains.

I change my riding habits as I have come to realize that every driver can be my killer. When I was young, walking facing oncoming traffic was the safe way, so I decided I needed to follow that advice and started riding against the traffic; this way, I have a fighting chance if a car drifts into the bike lane.

The morning is beautiful today, blue sky and a little bit of a tailwind, I am riding my freshly tuned Giant, the fastest bike that I have ever owned. On a flat surface, I have a maximum speed of just over 30 kilometers per hour. There is bumper to bumper vehicles on Rutland road due to construction at Reid's Corner; a car ahead of me moves into the bike lane, perhaps to see ahead. The only problem is that I am riding in the bike lane, and I react defensively, and I am forced off the road and prevent getting killed. I hit the first pothole hard, it slows me down a little, but I am unable to avoid the second. My front tire hits and comes to a sudden stop, and my body keeps going, flying over my handlebars through the air like superman only to hit the ground like a sack of potatoes. My hands are out in front of me to break my fall, the right side of my chest slams onto the hard-packed gravel.

I get up embarrassed and unable to breathe well; my front tire has a 90-degree bend in it, so I hold the front tire off the ground and continue my commute to work. I am bleeding from my knee, and both palms have gravel embedded under the skin. I contemplate going to the hospital, but I don't believe they will do much for a bruised lung; I hobble down the street with labored breath, I am in a lot of pain, but I am trying to hurry so I won't be late for work. I make it right on time; I am usually 30 minutes early; today is a prime example of why I give myself an extra 30 minutes to get to work. The following days are brutal, breathing hurts, coughing up blood, and laughter is exceptionally debilitating. Sleeping is tricky because I can only lay on one side, and getting out of bed is extremely painful. Riding a bike with a bruised lung is tough; still, I never missed a day.

I once had a girlfriend in Glenrosa, which is closer to Peachland than Kelowna; an hour and a half from my house. The bridge at the time barely had a place to walk and no place for a bike rider. I walked my bike across the bridge; I am walking on the narrow edge with my bike on the road, lifting it off the road each time a vehicle comes by. From the bridge to a steep, long climb, I am in full sweat by the time I reach the top on the other side. Near the trailer park, there is a magnetic hill, an optical illusion where the road looks level, but it is actually relatively steep. It is especially freaky coming back because I am not expecting to be going so fast. It is almost undetectable to vehicles as they are traveling at least 100 kilometers per hour through that area; it would be hard to experience if not on a bike. I almost didn't make it there, minutes before a car of four males sped by and threw a beer bottle at me, narrowly missing my head. They were speeding and drinking, driving at 140 kilometers per hour, the bottle flying towards my head is also traveling at 140 kilometers per hour; if it hit me in the head, I would be dead, the bottle would have exploded glass into my brain.

While people throw stuff at me all the time, it is not usually as dangerous as a beer bottle. The most popular thing is people like to flick their cigarette butts at me, it pisses me off, but it's not life-threatening unless one day it gets me in the eye. Apple cores, plastic bottles of urine are also popular, and all part of the motorists' disdain for bike riders; it is a game for the assholes to see if they can hit the bike rider. Half-way home one night, a white car with two males sped by me and threw a full large fast-food pop and hit me in the shoulder. It hurt like a punch in the shoulder and sprayed sticky syrup all over me, my bike, and backpack. I am angry enough that if I had a gun, I may have shot them, I calmed down soon after my shower, no physical harm done.

The bike lanes on the highway are hazardous; there is a possibility of death with every vehicle that passes. When a motorist hits a bike rider at 100 kilometers per hour, the bike rider dies, that is a fact. The creation of miles of bike paths were nothing more than changing the name form the shoulder of the road to bike path. The reality is these bike paths are only usable for bikes if a vehicle isn't using it. Bike lanes are the domain of drivers if they decide to turn right, to change a flat tire or engine failure. To look at a map, your kids are fighting; you need to use your cell phone. If a fire engine, police, or an ambulance requires you to pull over, give extra space to oncoming traffic, stopping to ask for directions, buying fruit on the side of the road. Every time a bus picks up a passenger, they pull into the bike lane and stop, I have narrowly escaped death from bus-drivers several times. Drivers accidentally drift into the bike lane because they are distracted by a cell phone, spilling coffee, changing the music, other traffic, putting on make-up because you're late for work, or maybe your kids are fighting. My point is that before it is declared a bike path, it should meet minimal safety criteria, and not subject a bike rider to potentially fatal collisions.

It takes me time to establish a route to work and back when I move to the city limits, 43 kilometers round trip; I am taking the highway because it is the most direct route. There is an overpass near the university turn off where the bike lane suddenly ends; there is no place to ride on the side of the road. I have nowhere to go, but into highway traffic, my speed is about 15 kilometers an hour, the posted speed is 80, but everyone is doing 100. Cars speed by me like I am standing still, dangerously stuck between the guard rail and speeding death. I ride as fast as I can to safety and meet up with the bike path on the other side of the overpass. I can't go through that every day, so the next day I try the other side of the highway, I am now riding against traffic, which takes something to get used to, it is much more nerve-racking to see the vehicles coming at, and past you at over 100 kilometers per hour.

The overpass has a significant incline that curves on the way up; drivers cruise this portion of the highway like they are playing a video game. Vehicles often drift into the bike path only to see me ahead and move back into their lane; one evening, I counted 14 times that a vehicle entered the bike lane on my way up.

It is sunny with a very heavy headwind; I am working hard at getting up the university overpass. I am three-quarters of the way up when I notice a semi-truck, blue cab and white trailer is in the bike lane ahead, I squeeze as far over as I can, I am not panicked as this happens all the time and the driver will see me and pull back out. He is going too fast and is drifting even further into my lane, my heart rate is already elevated from the hill and is increasing the closer the semi gets, I am trapped with nowhere to go. I ride along the embankment, making sure I don't touch it, or it will bounce my tire into traffic. Contact in milliseconds, I have no choice but to accept this is my fate, I am about to die, and this is going to hurt. As the length of the trailer portion rubs on my shoulder, I realized that I was going to get snagged at 100 kilometers an hour and dragged under into the tires. I wondered how long I would survive: if I am going to be conscious, with a mangled body bleeding out on the side of the highway.

Some people think that wind from the truck would suck you into the tires, but I can tell you that it is eerily calm, like a vacuum, no wind at all. There is a patch of gray dirt on my shoulder where the semi rubbed against me, I rode up to an area where I could pull over, I need to stop. I can't believe I am still alive; I feel numb, nauseous, and my body is trembling like a piece of my soul is missing. It takes a good five minutes to gather myself enough to carry on home.

I went home and pulled up a map; that is the last time I take that route. I will take back streets that take longer, but detour a large part of the highway, but still can't avoid suicide over-pass. My life depends on finding a new way, so even though the sign says no trespassing, I decide to go down the abandoned railway instead of risking being mangled on the highway. The metal tracks and wooden ties are gone, the gravel is loose and hard to pedal on, but it leads me to an industrial park. This route is longer and harder, but scenic, I ride by a small lake that I had no idea is there, hidden by a hill, it is not visible from anywhere else. There aren't any suitable alternatives, so this is my new way whether I like it or not.

My martial arts training gives me balance, quick reactions and awareness, and in combination with the safety rules I created, has kept me alive on the bike trails of Kelowna. My number one rule is avoid riding in front of a vehicle, I don't put my life in the hands of strangers. When a driver stops to wave me across, I decline and go behind them, basically avoid all possible contact at all times. Be aware of everything in eyesight, and pay special attention to any vehicle that enters the 20-foot danger zone that encompasses me. I anticipate that I might have to react quickly, being focused, and concentrating on staying alive. Do not expect motorists always to follow the rules of the road; if I didn't watch for pick-ups running red lights, I would be nothing but a stain on the asphalt 100 times over.

Vehicles will act erratically for no apparent reason; the driver could be drunk or high and speeding. The ever-increasing opioid addiction crisis means more impaired drivers on the street. I am at the mercy of the vehicles driving by, hopefully someone that isn't having a good day doesn't decide to take it out on me. Maybe it is an elderly person that has forgotten to take their medication and drifts just enough to kill me. All of the murderers that have yet to be found guilty and sentenced to prison next year are currently on the road with a weapon of opportunity. They can just say that I swerved in front of them and they couldn't avoid me. I wonder how many people have and will in the future, get away with murder, being that the cyclist is dead and can't testify. Every driver is currently in control of a weapon that could kill on a whim. Motor vehicles that don't signal are dangerous because they turn unexpectedly, signaling is important, but seems to be optional for most people, drivers are so lazy they literally can't lift a finger. Stay focused, alert, and don't drift off in thought, even if you don't get hit by a car, contact with anything at all will be very painful. Do not take crazy risks; I give myself extra time, so if I can't cross the street comfortably, I wait, I am never in a hurry to die.

Don't downplay the danger of making even the slightest contact with a vehicle. I knew a guy; he was riding down the street when he got hit by a car that was backing out of a driveway. He went to the hospital with a broken leg, and later that night, a blood clot entered his brain. He isn't dead, but is unable to speak, eat on his own or wipe his ass; the life he once knew, erased by a minor confrontation with the metal monster. A woman died here in Kelowna, when a car door opened into the bike lane, the car was parked and still claimed her life, her helmet didn't save her. Every year more names are piled onto the stack of dead bike riders murdered in the streets by the death machines.

Progress is slow and expensive when it comes to creating bike trails away from roads, but thankfully improvements are being made. The university path of a few hundred meters has a 1.9-million-dollar price tag: a strip of asphalt should not cost this much; there seems to be a lack of oversight. Bike lanes create a path to a viable future and should be a priority. We should be concentrating our efforts to designing trails that benefit the commuter cyclist rather than leisure riders. The gas emissions emitted increases every time a bike park is created outside the city, as people frequently drive their bikes to the park burning even more fossil fuel; that isn't baby steps; it is stepping backward. The people making the decisions with our tax dollars are not the ones biking to work and, therefore, unable to comprehend the subject; with no vision, there is no direction.

Chapter Seven
Fishing

I have gone fishing since I have been old enough to walk; without my truck, there were no more afternoons at the lake. Going fishing has created some of my favorite memories; trips that I took with my dad and grandpa are treasures I keep in a safe place deep inside my mind. When I was 17 my dad was managing a fly-in lodge in northern Manitoba, Lake Sasaginnigak has no roads the only way in or out was a pontoon plane. They call it a virgin lake, its purity is intact, and only experienced by the privileged few. One of the differences here is the massive size of the Northern Pike and Walleye; the accumulative weight in a week of fishing is staggering. Another way these fish stand-out is in how aggressive they are; if my hook is in the water, there is a fish on it.

My dad is busy helping a group of lawyers up from the States; wealthy men from across the border is the normal, the rate is $1,000 a day. They typically were high maintenance, amateurs requiring my dad spending more time with them. While the Americans occupy my dad's time, I take a boat and go out by myself; I find a honey hole just off the first point and the docks and drop anchor. I am pulling Walleye in one after another; I am allowed to keep six, I keep five of the biggest ones and will fill my limit if I snag one later while I am hunting Northerns. I have caught at least 30 in two hours; I am using a Pickerel rig, a few times I am catching two at a time. The wind has picked up and is now tossing me around, time for a break. I should have faced the boat away from shore before lifting the anchor, but I underestimate the wind, and the waves send me crashing into the rocks onshore. I am worried I will break the propeller if I start it in the shallow water, and I decide it would be better if my dad damaged the propeller, so I tied the boat and walked back, I am embarrassed, turns out I am as high maintenance as the rookies that just flew in. My dad handled the boat in the four-foot waves masterfully and beat me back to the dock with no damage except where I scratched it against the rocks.

A big complaint about eating Northerns is there are too many bones; the bones from a northern are a little thicker and longer than other fish, getting one stuck in your throat is very uncomfortable. My dad's Indian friend showed him a way to cut them that makes the meat virtually boneless. After skinning and removing the rack of bones on the inside of the fillet, make two incisions on either side of the main bone in the center, be sure not to cut straight through but stop at the next layer of bones, remove the one-inch strip and the center bone and all ones attached are also gone. Cut the boneless meat into medium pieces, coat them in a plastic bag of seasoned flour, then place in an inch of hot butter in a cast-iron frying pan, cook until golden and serve with my famous aioli sauce.

By six o'clock, the wind dies; the lake is calm, and it is time for Northern hunting, my dad steers the boat, he knows where to go. First, we have to take a trip to Garbage Island to deliver three five-gallon metal buckets of guts, each full to an inch from the brim. Imagine the worst thing you ever smelled, that smells like roses compared to fish guts that sit a day in the Manitoba sunshine in the summer. I am anxious to fight a big bad Northern and want to get this over with before I throw-up. I am trying to make-up for the boat mishap earlier when I offer dump the pails at the dumping site, which is up a hill and into the trees. It is two trips up a rocky slope, and I am trying not to get any on me, wasps swarm all around me, but they are focused on what I am carrying and leave me alone. The Deer flies are more interested in my flesh; they are fast and take a painful bite out of my arm. I could not leave Garbage Island fast enough, the most unpleasant experience of my life, until the next day when I made a solo trip with the honey bucket, that's a cute name for the bucket of the feces, not cute.

I was distracted by the buckets of fish guts and forgot the net; we are too far to go back for it. At most lakes, that wouldn't be a big deal; here, the Northerns are monsters, row after row of razor-sharp teeth with fangs that are an inch long. They look like a bad ass Barracuda with a scowl; the shape of its head makes it look like it's extremely pissed off at you. Years before, my uncle had a chunk of his leg taken by a seven pounder that he left unattended on the floor of the boat. Three of the Northerns caught today are over 15 pounds, one 17 the other 21 pounds, the record is 24 and a half pounds caught by my dad the year before. I think it might be fear that makes my heart jump when one of these monsters appears beside the boat; they look so scary.

At first, I thought it might be weeds, but then came the tug, and the fight is on. I am in no hurry to bring this one in; I need to tire him out a little if there is any chance of landing him. Sometimes they won't start fighting until they see the boat, not this one, he is angry and is determined to shake me free. The water is clear, and I can see him alongside the boat calmly swimming about three feet down, its enormous body flowing through the water with the powerful strokes of its tail, a 12 pound Northern. I try to lead him over to my dad, but he puts on a show and viciously tries to get off right in front of us. Once it settles down, I maneuver it over to my dad, where he clubs it, and while it is stunned, leans over the edge of the boat and plucks it out of the water by the gill plate, I guess we didn't need the net after all. I need a break for a minute, my arms are getting tired, so I reeled in, and while my hook was dangling over the side of the boat, a two-pound Pike jumps up, grabbing it out of the air; that is what I call fishing.

Trout fishing is not the same as Northerns or Walleye, as I realized after moving to Kelowna. British Columbia has the most beautiful mountain lakes, 100s of them, with the cleanest crystal-clear water ever seen. Trout are faster and have more fight than the fish I knew growing up on the prairies, above all else, they are the most intelligent of the freshwater fish. My tackle box that is full of the best lures, but I am no longer yielding my limit in fish. The Rainbow

Trout want nothing to do with my Canadian Wiggler, so I commenced to try every hook at the store, at every lake in my proximity.

At James lake, a red wedding ring with a trout killer spinner receives the most attention. It is very windy today, partly cloudy, it is bone-chilling cold out on the lake, with my knife I cut arm and head holes in a black garbage bag I brought with me, I slide it on like a t-shirt over my jacket to keep the wind out and get warm. Almost three hours of being tossed around like I'm on a carnival ride, and I have only caught two small ones that I released. I time my cast in between the gusts of wind, and get out my farthest cast of the day out towards the center of the lake.

I reel in a few turns and fish on; I could tell instantly that this is the a big one. The miserable weather melted away in the moment, replaced with the excitement the tug of war battle between me and my dinner. He leaps out of the water about three feet thrashing his head back and forth, trying to dislodge the hook. My heart sank in my chest when the line went slack; I started to reel in faster until I felt something, then nothing again. I finally realized it was charging at me; once a Rainbow gets slack in the fishing line, they will try to spit out the hook, I am bringing my line in as fast as I can. I am using light line, and my drag is set relatively loose, it proceeds to dive under the boat and up the shoreline, where my line gets tangled in the deadwood and weeds that line the shore. There is no pullback anymore; he has bested me; his determination to live has left me empty-handed and disappointed.

Fishing line is tangled up in the debris, about 30 feet of it, I wanted it and my wedding band back, but considered cutting it and avoiding the headache. The wind is bashing us against the logs at the shore, and it is too shallow for the propeller, it is a slow process as I run my hand along the line into the icy water and unwrap it from the branch in the pile of deadwood. The choppy waters and the wind make retrieving my gear slow, but I am making progress; I am glad I didn't cut so much off my brand-new line. I get to the end, and after one last untangle, I am free; to my surprise, there's my hook, and to my even bigger surprise, so is a beautiful two-pound Rainbow. He is still tired from about 30 minutes of fighting for his life; I lift him carefully from the water. He musters his energy for one more thrashing to escape certain death, his body jerks and shakes to get free and slips the hook from his lip. He is too late and falls to the floor of the boat, where lays a perfect specimen of a Rainbow Trout, pink blue black and silver. I considered throwing him back in, he fought so hard, and for so long, he probably deserved to live.

He was delicious, I make a tinfoil boat and place the fish, open side up, season with lemon pepper and dill, then slivers of red onion and garlic topped with pieces of butter, I put it on the barbecue for 20 minutes. All the bones are attached to the spine and can be removed with a skillful hand, leaving behind the tastiest and healthiest meat in the world. It tastes like salmon and has all the health benefits too, but this fish came from a mountain lake, far from the city; it has never seen pollution of any kind, not even gas motors are allowed on these lakes. That fish that lived its life in the cleanest water on the planet is now part of me; my body uses the energy from that fish to sustain life, therefore the saying, you are what you eat, and this meat makes me feel lean and healthy.

My eyes open and dart to my alarm clock, I have slept through my alarm, and my plans for the day, ruined. I was eyeing up a lake on Okanagan Mountain for years, last night I packed my gear so I could wake-up and go. This fishing trip is the first time I was going to a mountain lake on my bike; now, there isn't enough time. I need to arrive at the base at sunrise to give me enough time to get to the top and still have time to fish. I will have to push my long-awaited trip till next weekend. That night the air is electric, and a lightning strike starts a fire that the fire department attends to and put it out. A few hours later, Okanagan Mountain is on fire, it burns for three weeks, destroying 64,030 acres and 239 buildings. My ambitious plans to go fishing; delayed once again.

It's been a year since the great fire of 2003, a year that I spent disappointed that I slept in and missed a chance to see what Okanagan Mountain looked like before it burned up. I would not make that mistake again, setting two alarms. I woke five minutes before either went off and eagerly jumped out of bed. Not fire nor high water will keep me from going fishing, never so driven, I am unstoppable. The night lightens as it gives way to the dawn, I am on my way, so far everything according to plan. It seems to be a shorter distance when you are looking at a map; inches become miles. I have a special one, which details the lakes, but it is not a road map; I fail to take a turn where Lakeshore Drive becomes Chute Lake road. I realize my error, but not before climbing a substantial incline, so I backtrack, and I'm heading in the right direction again. There are plenty of sights to see along the water's edge, the wineries, the beaches, houses of the wealthy.

There are three or four vehicles in the gravel parking lot when I arrive at the base of Okanagan Mountain; I wonder if any of them are going to climb the mountain to go fishing. There is a wooden sign at the beginning of the trail, a rough map of the trails. I have no idea which one to take, but I choose the Banff Trail for no other reason than it is has a familiar name and I like Banff. Many people warned me not to do this because of how dangerous it is; I am wondering if anyone from the parking lot saw me disappear into the woods. It is quite steep, and I have to push my bike, I have ten one-liter water bottles in saddlebags, that add to the weight, my breathing quickens as I begin my fight against gravity. The trail is hard to follow; it is over-grown from lack of use; I lose the path and rely on my sense of direction. I am not lost; I just don't know where I am. The sun is not visible under the canopy of the treetops; it is still low in the morning sky. I keep going in the direction of up; I reason that if I continued up, I will eventually reach the top. I determined that the fire did not touch this part of the mountain because of how dense the forest is here.

There is a clearing ahead, I am relieved and head towards it, my weighted bike is difficult to push through the woods. I hit my shin against the pedal, the forest is thick, and when my bike stops suddenly, I end up walking into the metal spikes of my pedal and my right leg is bleeding a little. I would compare it to biting the inside of your cheek; it hurts like hell for a minute, then you do it again. There is a breeze when I get to the clearing; it cools my sweaty face; it is more comfortable to breathe out in the open; the air in the trees is heavy with moisture. Wild oats and other grasses are thick and as tall as my waist in places, as I move through this clearing, I am a little concerned that I might get bit by a Rattlesnake. Rattlesnake bites are frequent this year; many of the Okanagan hospitals are out of anti-venom, not that I could make it back to the parking lot in time anyway. Each nervous step for the next 50 feet, is accompanied with a plea to any listening snakes not to bite me. The forest thins out a bit, compared to the bottom portion of the mountain, and it isn't long after that I came across a small deer run, which I followed until I came upon the main trail. The trail I will use for all my future trips; it is a dry creek bed; the erosion marks show water still travels down here in the spring. The ten kilometers seems endless when fighting gravity every step of the way; my backpack weighs about 40 pounds and my bike and water another 50. I lost a lot of my legs in the dense forest when I lost my way, my quads are mushy, and I am sweating as much as I am drinking. I have to take a little break; I am questioning whether it's worth it and if I am on the right trail. I look up at the road ahead of me, take a swig of water and push ahead, one foot then the next foot repeat.

The brush alongside the trail has started to regrow since the fire; there are patches of mini wild strawberry plants. Wild chamomile is growing in select places, and I pick enough to make a cup of tea later, when I notice a king-sized four-leaf clover, shockingly I see that all the clover in this plant has four leaves. I picked three and carefully placed them in my saddlebag; I will press them in a book when I get home. The further up I went, the more evident that a beast of a fire tore through here. The forest is sparse with tall black charred sticks, and are providing no shade from the summer sun. On the other side of the path is a steep drop, I can hear rushing water far below, the trees on this side of the trail are practically growing on a cliff and seem mostly untouched. The path has become craggy; I have to be careful where I step, the loose rock makes it more difficult, and every few steps my footing gives way. Each time I around a corner, I hope it will be the last one, then it finally happens.

I am excited when I arrive at the top; the lake is not hard to find; it is only about 50 feet from the trail. Getting lost set, me back about two hours, so I needed to get my hook in the water as soon as possible. I reached the summit at 1:30, I wanted to give myself enough time to get off the mountain before dark, and I am not sure how long it will take to get down, so I decide to leave at 4:30. Divide Lake is narrow, standing on a cliff about 25 feet above the water, I cast halfway across. It all starts with a nibble; the trick is timing, jerk the rod back and set the hook into its top lip. It isn't long before my first fish, I am reeling it in, the cliff has sharp edges and small shrubs that appear to be growing out of the rock, and I don't want to get my line tangled in it. I manage to land her without incident, but she is too small; I can't drop her from this height, the impact from hitting the surface might injure her. I find a way down, jumping from boulder to boulder to the shoreline and release her back into the water, I move her body back and forth to get water passing over her gills, and she gently swims away and disappears into the lake. My next one is a keeper at 14 inches; I dislodge the hook and place my thumb against the roof of its mouth and snap its head back, severing its spine. It is a quick death, one last shiver of the body, then nothing. I then go down to where I released the first one and proceed to dress the fish. I make an incision into its belly, from head to anus, then I drag my finger hard against the spinal cord and remove all the guts in one move. I throw the intestines into the water, as is procedure when there is no fish cleaning station. From here, the fish sits in ice in my soft cooler I carried up in my backpack, when I get home, it is as fresh as the moment I caught it. I have my full limit in two hours, and I pack up with plenty of time to spare. I am sad to leave such an amazing place and wish I could stay longer; I take a last look around and one last breath of fresh mountain air before I start my descent.

Brakes were not an issue on the way up, now they are a matter of life and death. The brake pads were not at 100 percent before my descent and ground down to almost nothing in minutes. I try adjusting them and get a little more, but I have no choice but to drag my foot to slow me down, the loose rocks are bouncing me around like a Mexican jumping bean. My foot smashes against a bigger rock, and the pain is intense, I may have broken something, my speed increases and my limited brakes are doing nothing. Embedded in the path is a massive smooth white rock, and it launches me about 20 feet in the air. I am going way too fast and lose control as I try to negotiate the next bend, I clip a bush at the side of the trail and I get tossed from my bike. My backpack flies off of my shoulders, as I hit the ground my body begins to uncontrollable roll down the mountain. When I finally quit rolling, I let out a groan, I am hurt, but I am not going to stop here. I dust myself off and limp back up to my backpack and then my bike; I continue down with my right foot dragging, my left foot throbbing. I am careful not to build up too much speed because once I get going too fast, I cannot stop, I end up walking my bike down the very steep parts. The path comes out of the forest at the end of Timberline road; I am making mental notes for future fishing trips, I pass a goat farm and a large boulder with a badger hole under it; I am without a doubt coming back, and this time I will be better prepared.

I make plans to go again in two weeks; my thoughts of Okanagan Mountain consume me; I have solved my fishing dilemma most incredibly. I found a place with great fishing, where I could go on my bike, and for a bonus, motor vehicles can't. I bought a new bike, one with disc brakes, what a difference they make. This time I know exactly where to go and what to expect, I am pushing myself, I slow down to catch my breath but don't stop until I reach the lake. Oblivious to my body, my brain overrides any cramps or fatigue issues, and I reach the summit in four and a half hours, my best time ever. It is 10:30 am; I have more than six hours so that I can fish more relaxed.

This trip is my second time to Divide lake, and I have yet to see another living soul besides at the parking lot. I guess no one wants to climb ten kilometers to go fishing when they can drive their SUV to any of the other amazing lakes in the Okanagan. I have already caught a Rainbow when I decide my clothes are so cold and wet from sweat that I need to hang them to dry. I get naked, confident that I am all alone here; I hang my clothes in the sun on a nearby bush. I have never fished nude before, it remarkably feels exciting and freeing, and then you add in the thrill of catching a rainbow, I am on the top of the world. Until the most massive bug I have ever seen buzzes by me, suddenly I want my clothes back, I am hoping I don't get stung in the genitals. Then another one buzzes by me, and I become a little freaked out as I realize there is a swarm of them.

Before I could grab my shorts, I make an astonishing discovery, hovering in front of me is a Hummingbird checking me out. His family joins him, and soon there is a flock of

Hummingbirds all hovering around me. I stood perfectly still as not to frighten them away; they are continuing to hang around me and are coming closer. They seem as curious of me as I am of them, I have never seen a flock of hummingbirds and judging by the lack of fear they have, they have never seen anything like me either. Here I am, naked, fishing off a cliff, surrounded the cutest creatures you have ever seen; it is transcendent, my heart swells, as I stand there astonished by Mother Nature. If I had a million dollars, I would spend it on those five minutes. They hover a little and fly away, then come back; at one point, there is at least eight hovering around me. A rainbow decides to eat my hook, and the action startles the little guys, and one by one they fly away, until only one remains, he stays for a few seconds longer perhaps to say good-bye; I never see another

Hummingbird on any of my subsequent trips.

An hour had passed since I hung my clothes out to dry; they are dry enough, and being naked outside is getting old. If I push my luck, someone will come along while I am down cleaning a fish, or maybe I will get stung on the genitals. I get dressed and fish the rest of the day, catching at least 20 and releasing all but my limit. The Hummingbirds touched me profoundly, and I still felt kind of foggy, like I was in a magical haze. In the following years, I may have mentioned my adventures a few times, and I guess I got a buddy interested because he wanted me to take him there. I warned him that it is not the most leisurely climb, but he reassured me it couldn't be worse than football practice. I have had crazy intense football practices as well, so I agreed.

I am waiting outside my house when my buddy pulls up and parks in front of my house. We should be halfway there by now, so I am anxious to get going, but it is a beautiful day, nothing but blue skies. It takes longer to get there; buddy is slowing me down; he is not an experienced bike rider. He also didn't bring any water, I guess he thought there would be water stations, but it is not that kind of park. There are no souvenir stores along the way, nowhere to buy an overpriced bottle of water for five bucks. As pure as the lake and streams are, they are not safe to drink from unless you purify it first. I always bring extra water when venturing into the wild, just in case. Buddy is drinking my water like a fish and is needing a rest every 20 feet, it is taking too long, and I am growing impatient. He reassures me that he will be fine if I go ahead so that I can get some more fishing time. I motored up the last two kilometers; I am still fresh, I barely exerted myself so far. I have three fish on ice when he makes his appearance at the lake; I am relieved that he didn't turn back or get eaten by a bear. I am also happy for him to have made it, even though he is now lying on the ground motionless. While buddy has a rest, I continue catching fish, and soon my cooler is stocked with fresh Rainbows.

Coming down the mountain is more challenging than you would think, but it is steep in a lot of places, and it is easy to get going too fast. I am leading the way down when he whizzes by me, leaves the trail, and disappears over the edge; I am hoping he is not dead. I cannot see him, so I get off my bike and start climbing down the steep slope; I find him behind a boulder; he is hurt but can still walk. I help him back up to the path and trade bikes with him, the handlebars bent, the front tire is wobbly, and the brakes are out. Halfway down, he starts vomiting; he might have a concussion; the important thing now is to get back to civilization. His energy is fading, and it takes a lot of coaxing, but we get back to my house: I give him a couple of Trout for his trouble, and he is on his way. Once at home, he can rest and brag to his wife about how he fell off the side of a mountain, narrowly escaping death. I had a great day; besides the lengthy travel time, I spent more time getting there and back than I did fishing.

I wanted to camp up there for a couple of nights, so I could spend more time relaxing as the day trips were all business. A co-worker wanted me to take him up there, so I planned a three-night camping trip to Divide Lake. This buddy is in great shape, a marathon bike rider that is currently training and looking for a challenge. A former Boy Scout, I am always prepared, I have a checklist I created, so I never forget anything. This trip, I will have to pack light, so I leave the cast iron pan at home; but I ended up bringing the kitchen sink. My inflatable boat weighs the most, and it is the most important as I want to explore more of the lake, to see how the fishing is in the other parts I can't get to by land. My bike trailer is overflowing, I tarp and strap it, I estimate the weight to be around 200 pounds before my backpack, saddlebags, and bike.

The wheels of my bike trailer look stressed out; I am a little worried they won't stand up to the rigors ahead. It is sluggish starting up, but once I get moving, it is manageable, but it takes quite a bit out of me at the hills. By the time I ride the 25 kilometers from my house to the base, my legs are mushy, I get a half kilometer into the forest, and I need a break. I woke an hour later faced with the realization of the possible impossible journey; as it gets steeper, I will get to a point where I am physically unable to push or pull the weight. Buddy lights up a joint and we discuss our options, we could call it off and go home, I could leave the trailer and just go for the afternoon, or buddy could ride ahead, then walk back and together push the trailer up. I didn't want to waste my requested time off from work, and I felt invigorated after my nap; he is here looking for a challenging workout.

For the next 12 hours we pushed my bike trailer up the mountain, we had to stop and camp on the trail because it was dark and could no longer see where we were going. I brought a jug of frozen orange juice and vodka; I could feel it flow down my dry, cracked throat, and into my stomach. We build a fire and cut sticks to roast hot-dogs and marshmallows; I was eating trail mix on the way up, but I am starving. My dog is plump and is sweating its juices, that is how you know it's ready; I brought buns, all the condiments, and am always happy to share. Food tastes better when you are starving; drink tastes better when you are parched. Now that my stomach is full with campfire delicacies; I need some much-needed sleep. I crawled into my tent and passed out, the next thing I know it is morning, and my bladder is full, time to get up.

We break camp quickly; I don't want to spend another second on this trail; I would rather be fishing. It takes another four hours to get to the lake with the steepest and craggiest stretches near the top; the trailer continues to get caught on the large rocks, so we have to lift the trailer over it. The lake is a welcome sight, and I have my hook in the water about five minutes after we get there, I am here exclusively for the fishing. Buddy goes exploring; he didn't bring any fishing gear and is more interested in checking out the summit. I catch a two-pound Rainbow while he is gone, the largest I ever caught at Divide Lake. I also use the alone time to grab a bar of soap and go skinny dipping to wash the trail off me; I swim out to the center of the lake and back. The water is cold but refreshing; the afternoon sun is warm on my skin as I lather up onshore then swim back out to rinse off.

I feel like a million bucks; I am fishing at a frantic pace, almost every cast a fish, we are feasting on Rainbows tonight. I season six trout in tinfoil boats, line them up on a strip of wood I split with my ax, and strategically place them on the white-hot coals. After dinner, the bones and skin burnt in the fire, the only evidence of our feasting is our bloated bellies. I can barely fit down a couple of roasted marshmallows before I am ready to pass out.

Buddy didn't bring a tent; he intended to sleep under the stars; the first night, he slept by the fire and was at a lower altitude. The temperature drops drastically when the sun goes down on the summit, I thought he would be uncomfortable sleeping out in the open, and with the wind picking up, I offered to share my tent, he declined the offer for about 20 minutes.

Waking up at Divide Lake was perfect, the morning crisp and sunny, I started a fire to make coffee. I have a campfire peculator that makes coffee so good that every sip I take I can't believe how good it is, I have three cups before I take my boat out. I put on a life jacket, I am not sure what to expect, and there is not much shore to swim to, I could feel a strong current the day before when I went for a swim. One side is rocky cliffs, the other dense deadwood 20 feet out from shore. The lake gets narrower and shallower; I don't want to chance continuing in my inflatable boat, I would have kept going if I was in an aluminum. I catch fish everywhere in that lake, but there is no place better than the cliff I have been fishing. The boat turns out to be unnecessary but puts my mind at ease, knowing there isn't a hidden honey hole holding monster Rainbows somewhere else in the lake.

I take a break from fishing to shoot my guns; two matching Russian made air pistols that look like a 9mm, I modified them with laser sights. Unfortunately, powered by CO2 cartridges, the seals couldn't handle the extra pressure due to the altitude, so that was short-lived. I returned to fishing where I am pulling one in every five minutes, I have caught more fish than I can count. It looks like it is Rainbows for dinner again, and that's perfectly fine for me.

I woke at dawn; we will be heading home today; after coffee, I break down the tent and start packing up. There is still some ice in my cooler, although most of it has melted; it's okay, I needed the space for 18 decent sized Rainbow trout, my limit for three days. When I get home, I will place each fish into a large zip-lock bag, fill it with water and freeze, this method assures no freezer burn, thaw it out in the sink, and it is fresh as the moment it was caught. I pack up everything back in my bike trailer; I am eager to get home, I burned out from fishing.

We leave before noon; buddy is antsy about going, he has had enough of the mountain. The two hundred pounds behind me is now bearing down on me, forcing me down against my will. When I brake, the trailer pushes me over, and I wipe out about ten times on the way down. I am frustrated and tired by the time I ride out of the forest; I just want to get home, have a shower, and sleep for 24 hours. When I did get to my house, I find out that my baseball team is unable to replace me, and I will have to play. I shower, ride ten kilometers to make the 7:00 pm start, I pitch a one-hitter and hit four for four.

Those four days allowed me to test my metal and gave me perspective on how much I can put my body through. I compare any distance I ride to the limits I endured on that trip. That was also the last time I ever went fishing; my desire decreased as my empathy for animals increased. It grew harder for me to view Rainbow Trout as only meat, but a living creature that is swimming around living life. The truth is, I even have a hard time killing a worm, a far cry from the mighty hunter of my youth.

Chapter Eight
Road kill

I spot something ahead on the shoulder of the highway; it looks like a hat, maybe it blew out of a pick-up that was moving household items. As I get closer I can see that the hat is made from fur, I am not sure how I feel about fur hats, but I remember I wanted one as a kid; I decide that I will pick it up and take it with me and determine how I feel about it later. I slow down and pull up beside my new winter hat, and make a startling realization; this is not a hat. I feel sadness swell up in my chest; the fur looks like a small piece of sod folded up on the highway. There is no face, no feet, no tail, nothing to identify what kind of animal it was, only a mangled clump of fur with a small half circle pool of blood coming from underneath. I think it must be a cat, maybe a beaver, or a raccoon, whatever it was, it died violently.

It is a beautiful day to be alive today; it is warm at sunrise; the air is still; a perfect day for a bike ride. I live by the Quail Ridge golf course; it is exceptionally green today, perfectly groomed, the groundskeeper has his dog with him today. I ride along in my shorts and a t-shirt taking in the sights and enjoying the sun on my face; I feel good about the day's outlook. There is only a handful of vehicles on the road this early, and I fly to the highway, there are flashing lights ahead, looks like the police. It's a roadblock, with the traffic redirected to a single lane, I decide that is not for me as I breeze through the barricade. A young male deer is laying on its side, there is fur on his tiny antlers, from my angle it doesn't look that bad. I half expect him to wake up, maybe he is only stunned and will jump up and scamper away. Seeing the other side of him makes it certainly fatal; chunky bloody guts lay on the highway. I wonder if he was running with other deer when he got killed, it must have been a semi that hit him use there are no signs that a vehicle was involved at all, only a large truck could hit a deer with no damage. The police are waiting for clean up, they bring street cleaners, and by the time I ride by on my way home, it was like it never happened.

I am not a fan of snakes, but I feel bad when one dies on the road, this one has a tire track right in the middle of its body, food for crows now. The next week it is a pretty yellow baby bird laying near the curb on the freshly cut grass. I once saw a baby raccoon try to wake up its mother at the intersection of Enterprise and Dilworth. Sometimes the dead are removed right away, either by crows or city workers; other times, I ride by a carcass every day until it has decomposed. The body of a female duck laid on the side of the highway for months until it became flat and disintegrated into the gravel, I would still look at that spot when I rode by, even after it was gone. There was a dead juvenile cat on Rutland road near the church that lay in the bike lane for two weeks until one day, two boys placed it on the grass on the other side of the sidewalk and covered it with dry sticks. It snowed soon after that, but I knew the cat was still there.

At the end of Innovation drive, where it connects with university drive lays a hawk or an owl, there is no head. I am thinking how disappointed a taxidermist would be had the massive bird be found by one. For the next three weeks I wonder if it is there when I ride by, I am surprised that no one has seen such a large bird, it seems to have moved each day slightly; the crows are probably picking at it. It lays wings spread wide, and I create scenarios of how it died, maybe a mouse was scurrying across the road, and the second its talons pierce into dinner, a truck makes deadly contact and sends into the ditch. There will be no more majestically soaring high in the sky; the babies back at the nest will starve and die. Instead, the once-mighty predator lays lifeless on the side of the road, dinner for maggots and scavengers.

I am on my way home; a beautiful, strong tailwind caresses my back as I cruise down the highway. I take a left at Airport way, almost home, I come around the corner fast, and I am surprised to see two badgers trying to cross the four lanes. They were half-way across when I intruded on their daring run for it; the female stopped in her tracks when she saw me. She looks at me frozen in fear, I slowed and started to ride out into the road to block any vehicles that might come along. The male Badger is nudging her on the shoulder, urging her to continue to the other side, I tell her it's okay to go ahead. The two scampers off, and I feel like I have had a cute moment with nature.

I had seen a large animal hole dug in the dirt in the quarry; now, I know whose home it is. The quarry is only temporary, while they build the community of Quail Ridge. Now finished, part of the gravel pit is designated to be a parking lot, and the Badger's home is destroyed to make room for progress. That is why the pair of Badgers are crossing the road in the early evening; they are looking for a suitable location to build a new home. The following days I told the story to anyone who would listen, the human-like actions I had witnessed by the most adorable couple. Now that I knew they were in the locale, I was actively looking for them, hoping to get another moment.

About two weeks went by, and I had all but given up, then lo and behold right in middle of the highway is one of the Badgers, only is face up and not moving. Sadness overwhelmed me as I rode by, I wondered if it was the female, and she if got startled and froze up like she did in our encounter. I see a dead Gopher almost every day, and it's sad but doesn't affect me; seeing one of my Badger friends a victim of a vehicular homicide, left me both sad and angry. I was still disturbed two days later when I came across the other Badger, dead in almost the exact spot as his deceased mate. Emotion overcame me, and I tried not to cry when I realized that he couldn't live without her and killed himself.

I can't imagine how many animal deaths occur in North America if my little stretch of highway is an indicator. What I know for a fact is there was not any roadkill before motor vehicles, and they continue wreak havoc on wildlife.

Chapter Nine
Good Intentions

It might surprise you to know that in the 20 years, riding every day, I never once wore a bike helmet. I have worked jobs that require I be presentable and having helmet-head hair all day is not an option. I have never needed one, the police leave me alone, and in the few wipe-outs I have had, my head was not injured or in harm's way. A helmet is an unnecessary requirement that is deterring the average commuter from riding a bike as transportation. The only permanent injury I have sustained is hearing loss in my left ear from an ambulance siren.

The only ones who benefit from the helmet law is the auto industry and the sports shops. I consider any act that prevents a no pollution solution a crime against humanity. I think what happened in this instance is the people that introduced the helmet law used statistics from bicycle stunts, a craze for getting famous on YouTube. You should wear protection if you are doing jumps and flips, but an experienced rider is in no danger of getting hurt riding down a path.

These members of the government are most likely the same ones that changed legislation to make a bicycle classify as a motor vehicle. It should be obvious, a bike does not have a motor is not a motor vehicle, which makes me question how out of touch are these politicians. By changing some wording, the government created 100s of kilometers of bike paths without lifting a finger, now that they designated bicycles as motor vehicles, they can legally ride on the shoulder alongside their fellow motorist. Incidentally, bike riders were already doing that. A helmet will not protect my life against a real motor vehicle traveling at 100 kilometers an hour. Maybe they had good intentions, or perhaps it's the oil companies trying to make biking less appealing.

The proverb, the road to hell, is paved with good intentions, translates to mean sometimes you want to help but end up making things worse. Good people started the recycling initiative because plastic and metal take so long to decompose, causing landfills to overflow. Paper products and tin cans are recycled enthusiastically, it is an easy way to save a tree, but it does very little if anything to improve the environment. The public is doing their part, and it is not their fault the recycle, reduce, and reuse program is such a monumental failure. The blame here goes to the government; they are ultimately responsible for the handling of the collected product.

I make sure to rinse my plastic milk jug, and I turn it upside down in the sink, throw the lid in the garbage; unclean recycling attracts insects and can make a whole shipment contaminated and unusable. I throw it in the blue bin and bring it to the curb, then a three-ton truck comes up beside it and hydraulically lifts the container and dumps it in the back. Then after collecting all of the neighbors' recycling, it is taken to a sorting plant, they sort the plastic, metal, and paper, then transported again to a designated destination. My milk jug is transported to another country and joins a mountain of my past milk jugs. When GPS tracks the movement of random parcels of plastic, it shows that only one in four milk jugs get converted into pellets suitable to create other plastic products. The others end up in a landfill, or we pay other countries to take it. The harmful effects of transporting and transforming plastics back to basic form makes it more damaging to the earth if you recycle.

The truck that picks up your recycling burns fuel that poisons the air was not there until the recycling program. Employees of the sorting plant drove their vehicles to work; then, more trucks deliver to the corresponding destination. Ships are some of the biggest polluters; they transport your recycling somewhere else, out of sight, out of mind. It is frustrating when I think extra steps to dispose of garbage is all in vain; my good intentions are in truth destroying our earth. I still recycle but put more emphasis on re-purposing, I hope that the process will improve; meanwhile, I realize that at best, it has no positive results for the planet.

The reduce part is redundant since the primary intent is to reduce the amount of garbage bags, and now we have reusable bins. The bins are a step forward, even though manufacturing these had a significant impact on the environment, the long term it is a positive. What some people overlook is that there is much more environmental damage making reusable items. You must use your reusable bag 120 times to equal the same harmfulness to the environment as one plastic grocery bag, if you don't get 120 uses; you are hurting the planet. I re-purpose all of them; they line my garbage or carry an extra pair of shoes or line my winter boots, now you will have to use your reusable bag 240 times to equal one dual purpose plastic bag. If we abolish the grocery bag, I would have to purchase separate bags which increases production, causing even more pollution. The bottom line is using a reusable bag for your groceries is not better; reusable products have to last longer, which requires more manufacturing and results in more environmental impact.

I have the biggest problem with the single-use plastic crusaders, a prime example of the road to hell is paved with good intentions. They see an island of plastic floating in the Pacific and Whales dying from ingested grocery bags and their solution is to rid the world of single-use plastic. Not only is this unrealistic; I wouldn't want a slushy or a milkshake without a straw, as we know, the environmental impact to make reusable straws ultimately has a negative impact. When I finish with my straw, I throw it in the garbage, the garbage truck picks it up and takes it to the dump, there it decomposes within a few weeks. I know this because People throw their garbage out the window of vehicles, and it litters the side of the highway. Every day I ride by the same straw and watch it decompose, after two weeks it has splintered into tiny pieces, at three weeks it is unrecognizable. The anti-straw crusaders would have you believe that somehow, my straw has ended up in the ocean, even though I live in Kelowna that has no connecting waterways. Maybe they think people are driving four hours to walk down to the Pacific Ocean and throw their straw in.

The straw people like the scarecrow in the wizard of Oz, have no brains; although they have the best intentions, they have a disability, they are unable to think things through. There is only one logical way these straws are ending up floating in an island the size of Texas, and that is in the garbage. Companies are offering to dispose of your trash, but are taking the money then dump it in the ocean. The floating straws and plastic bags are proof of that, and without these tell-tale signs, these criminals could continue undetected. If I was a conspiracy theorist, I might think perhaps the people making a fortune by dumping illegally, actually orchestrated the straw ban as it benefits them the most. Straws are not being thrown in by themselves; no one is driving to the coast to throw in a handful of straws. Batteries, diapers, dirty kitty litter, dog poop, and all the improperly disposed dregs are also added to this unappetizing soup we call our oceans. The guy down the street tosses containers of dirty motor oil in or some other item he might have to pay to dispose, next door to that guy, a woman throws out her broken laptop. The straws are indicators that may save the entire human race, which makes the anti-straw people a threat to our existence. I believe that they have the best intentions, but their shortsightedness could kill us all.

I think it is common knowledge that we cease to exist if our oceans die, so every effort should be made to protect them. We need to identify these criminals that jeopardize the precious lives of your children; regular and random GPS tracking should be a requirement for all coastal cities in the world. Eventually, all garbage needs tracking procedures as a safety precaution; these checks need to be scrutinized by different branches of government in efforts to avoid corruption. The penalty for dumping in any waterway anywhere in the world should command the most severe punishment, considering their actions are threatening humanity. If it were up to me, I would impose monumental fines, complete seizure of all money and assets of everyone associated with the crime and a sentence of life in prison for anyone that gained financially. It may sound too harsh, but could be effective as a deterrent, if they are allowed to continue it would result in the death of everyone in the world.

I am sure that the invention of the automobile was with good intentions, welcomed by all as one of humankind's greatest achievements. The truth is, it has desecrated our planet, oil spills plague the earth, devastating ecosystems, and taking millions of animals' lives. Drilling is destroying many areas in the ocean; fracking contaminates freshwater supplies, not to mention all of the massive oil spills that have been occurring for decades; oil companies are responsible for an unimaginable loss of wildlife. When you see a baby bird struggling to breathe and slowly die from an oil slick, you should know that it is happening because of you are driving, you might as well have poured oil on that innocent life yourself. Motorists are more dangerous and caused more loss of life than any faction in the history of humanity. They continue to destroy the planet with complete disregard for life and the diseases it causes. Vehicles are responsible for all illnesses and death that could be prevented by exercise. It is no coincidence that the country with the most cars also has the most obese and ill people in the world; their overwhelmed health care system is a direct effect of the invention of the automobile.

If your logic is that everyone else is doing it, you should quit acting like you're in high school and realize that if ten men beat on another man and that person dies, even by accident, then all ten men will be consequently be convicted of murder in a court of law. Therefore, it doesn't matter if you drive a little or a lot, if you belong to the mob of people that kills just one person; you are all guilty. It must be so surreal to realize you are not just a killer, but a mass serial killer; it is just another atrocity committed by the human race. We can't imprison the millions of killers, but you can't let the culpable go free. The crime of manslaughter can't go unpunished just because so many people are doing it. No one will volunteer guilt, so they are allowed to murder with impunity, despite the World Health Organization's report that states automobiles are responsible for some cancers. No one is interested, but when the World Health Organization accuses you of murder and no one bats an eye; we are in trouble. There should be consequences for committing such heinous crimes, and should warrant maximum punishment. There are too many to incarcerate, but there still must be punishment for their participation in crimes against humanity. The only answer is to convict each member at the World Court and hang every member of the most destructive group of humans the world has ever known.

Of course, I am not sincere about any of that; my intention is to emphasize that our survival depends on clean air in our thin layer of breathable atmosphere. The saints of the world are driving, kind considerate people with love in their hearts and would never intentionally hurt anyone. Motorists are merely victims of the oil companies, and the auto industry who are controlling the governments and thus the citizens of many countries. The motorist is hypnotized by flashy commercials as it glorifies the next hot vehicle; you buy it so you can satisfy your need to be better than your neighbor. I know even the world's best people, who have performed acts of kindness and only have good intentions, drive, and don't deserve any blame. I believe these people would stop driving if the government announced that motorists are responsible for the millions of cases of cancer. Which makes the situation impossible; the government might collapse if suddenly revenue from oil taxes cease. The only way to save us is to stop driving at an individual level; if each person takes responsibility for their pollution.

My vision of the future is companies with fleets of electric cars, when you need to go somewhere, they deploy one to you with tap of your phone. When your vehicle arrives, you will notice that there is no driver, a car that cannot get in an accident. With computerized navigation, go ahead and talk on your phone, watch a show, eat or relax. Your car is also detailed each time it returns for a recharge, so it's like a new car every trip. This is only practical if the electricity used to power the fleets of cars is generated by damns and not by burning coal. A hydroelectric damn creates power without infecting the air, the electricity is made by gravity, when it forces water through the turbines.

Having a vehicle is a burden for the average person; financially, you pay for the original purchase, insurance, fuel, tires, repairs, general maintenance, traffic violations, and hopefully, things don't go bad after an accident. Giving up ownership of your car also frees up the time spent on filling up at the pump and car washes and other hours admiring her. I find it odd that people drive to the gym to ride a bike, riding to work would save time, money and the environment. If the average person could ride a few times a week, it would take a lot of pressure off the healthcare system; I think everyone would agree exercise is key to a healthy life.

We are only alive because of the thin layer of oxygen encasing the earth, which is there mostly because of the massive amounts of water on the planet. The ice that keeps the oceans at temperatures able to sustain life is melting; once they are gone, so are we, the countdown has begun. It is quite baffling that humans have taken such a cavalier attitude towards the things that keep us alive. In the future, I envision a world law that establishes a zero-tolerance for contaminating water or air and is strictly enforced.

Chapter Ten
Good vs Evil

My dream was to open my own restaurant, and after years of hard work, working two full time jobs and saving everything I could, I opened a small cafe. I sink everything I have into it, inducing all available credit, I am all in for my dream. I leave my house at 5:30 am with my bike trailer in tow, and I am at Superstore five minutes before they open. I buy supplies for the day, and make it to the cafe in plenty of time to open at 7:00. I make a daily soup from scratch, and my burgers are made from a ground chuck, sirloin blend. I prepare all the meals; I am told I am a very good chef.

Things were great the first six years, until the building my restaurant is in is sold. When they change the locks, they don't give me a key, they tell me the cleaners will unlock the doors in the morning and lock up at night. I am not happy about not being able to access my business any time I want and I express my displeasure. A few months go by and I mention it several times with no response, and I am tired of being locked out of my restaurant, waiting for the janitor to let me in. Frustration got the best of me and in a moment of poor judgment, I decide to withhold rent until I get a key. I think maybe I was played and this is planned, because they immediately sent bailiffs in to seize the property. I didn't have enough money to relocate and my dream died.

All men have sin, where they differ is some men have more than others, and sometimes we sin for justified reasons; almost everyone will steal bread to feed your starving family. I wonder how many would go through with it, if the stolen bread belonged to a family that will starve to death because of this understandable sin. I hear some say God does not exist, merely an improbable fantasy; stories passed down from generation to generation that have lost their influence over time. Lessons for children so that they behave out of fear; guidelines for adults so they can co-exist with other adults. For the nonbelievers, there is no need to worry about consequences for heinous acts, because when you die, it's lights out, fade to black.

Cultures from around the world have one thing in common; their civilization has a religion, sometimes multiple. Christian, Hindu, Muslim, Jewish, and all the others have at least one thing in common; they believe there is something after death. Whether angels or virgins await you or you come back as a butterfly, what gives the world peace is the knowledge that this life is not the end.

When I was young, I liked going to Sunday school; I loved the stories. My favorite, a man with incredible strength, the source of his power, his hair. His girlfriend reveals his secret to the bad men, who cut his hair, and he loses his super strength. He then asks God for his power back for one last act of revenge against the bad men. At least that is how I remember it; I was five or six, and it was the last time I went to church regularly. We all know that the son of God could walk on water and turn water to wine, but that doesn't impress me, I have seen at least two magicians do it.

The Tooth Fairy, the Easter Bunny, Santa, and God filled my imagination with magic, until I hit seven. Let me get this straight; the Tooth Fairy is just mom slipping a quarter under my pillow. The Easter Bunny didn't hide chocolates around the house, and Santa didn't eat the milk and cookies. God is real, though; he killed Tiger, my cat that ran on to the highway. As I got older, it seemed apparent that God is another story told to children.

According to my grandmother, God blessed me with common sense, and that I am lucky because a lot of people don't have it. I placed my faith in science; facts and logic make sense. Watching the television show, The Big Bang Theory made me curious about string theory. It fascinated me, and my thirst for knowledge of quantum physics consumed my thoughts. As humans, we have yet to understand how enormous something can be; we don't know where the end of our ever-expanding universe is, or if our universe is just one of millions. Ignoring the technological aspect of it, even the smallest particle can theoretically be split in half, and so on for infinity. There are many things we still don't understand, but we are getting closer to understanding our world. I would learn about the vibrating filaments, quarks, four fundamental forces. Then I found God, not in a spiritual way, but in an, I can give you directions kind of way.

The world's top physicists have been working on string theory and variations of it for the last three decades; the math is beautiful, but cannot be physically proven. Unproven does not mean it isn't right; we can't give substance to love either, but we know it exists, and I choose to trust that the most brilliant minds on the planet are going to be correct sometimes. My main interest is the dimensions, ten dimensions, plus a dimension of time. You probably think this is some made-up fiction, but no, there are 11 dimensions according to the latest string theory called m-theory. The math won't work with five dimensions or any other random number, and it works beautifully with 11. Scientists think our gravity is so much weaker than it should be because these dimensions are sharing it with us. Each one has unique properties; God lives in the tenth dimension, where a being would control all time and space from the beginning of time till the end of time.

The law of Conservation of Energy is as follows; the total energy of an isolated system is constant. Energy is neither created nor destroyed; it can only be transformed from one form to another or transferred from one system to another.

There are three types of energy in the human body; heat, kinetic, and stored, perhaps there is a fourth and the soul or id is energy. Therefore, as the laws of science state, energy can never die. I believe that our energy represented by the soul will transform into another form, capable of being absorbed by the next dimension. A scientist once claimed the body lost 21 grams at the time death; further experiments conducted to see if there is any weight loss concluded no difference. I am not sure how much a memory weighs, but I would guess right around the same as love and belief.

Strange things happen in the world of quantum physics; an example is the double-slit experiment. In this experiment, there are two screens; the front screen has two slits in it. A single atom shot at the first screen, it goes through one of the slits and is detected on the back screen. After a while, a design emerges, known as the Disruption Pattern. When a detector observes this experiment, the atom's behavior changes, evident in the pattern on the back screen. Turning off the sensor, and the Disruption Pattern returns. From this experiment, we can conclude the being observed alters an atoms behavior.

If looking at something can physically change its behavior, then what about belief. A lucky jersey worn by a fan might give the team that extra inch for the win, or if your team loses, the team needed more than an inch. If someone believes in a diet, it is because it is working for them, but maybe it is the belief that makes it work for them, because the diet doesn't work for everyone. Believe in yourself and good things will happen; belief in a placebo may actually cure you. If observing an object can affect change, then what impact does faith and love have in the physical world. Religions are different because of how they interpret the afterlife; according to string theory, the world will unite because all religions are right.

There are many types of energy in the universe, such as kinetic, stored, heat, dark, mechanical. When you die, your energy becomes stored energy, ready to be consumed by the earth. The amount of energy in a soul could be undetectable to humans; in fact, the entire dimension could be smaller than an electron. My soul or id is energy, and it can never die; when I do, if my belief is absolute, if I am confident that I am a decent person, and if my desire is strong enough, I pass over to the other side. I know deep down that if I am worthy, my soul will enter a new world. Those with no direction will be lost in eternal nothingness or will indeed fade to black. Faith in God is the intelligent choice; if you believe, you go to heaven; if you don't, there is nothing for you. If there is no afterlife, you won't know either way; there will be no one to laugh at you or rub it in your face; if God doesn't exist, you won't know it. Religions are different because of how they interpret the afterlife; if string theory is right, there will be no more religious wars because all religions might be true.

Good and evil are not decided in a courtroom but inside the hearts of humankind. The battles to determine innocents or guilt take place everywhere, but nowhere like the United States of America. The news covers it 24 hours a day, and we all soak it in on the big screen. Sometimes it is hard to know who the bad guys are, because they will always tell you that they are the good guys. In a court of law, the guilty almost always plead innocent in hopes of getting away with it. We all know a famous football player that got away with a bloody vicious double homicide and is now golfing instead of rotting in prison.

The rich don't have to follow the rules like poor people do; they hire legal teams made up of the highest-paid lawyers and evil triumphs. A person that doesn't have money, has a public defender, an innocent person might be found guilty, or someone may get a lengthy sentence for a minor crime. There are many cases where men were found not guilty after decades of incarceration, this is how a court of law sentences torture for the innocent. I wonder if that judge feels regret, or does he callously shrug it off, and how he would feel if he accidentally got locked up for 20 years.

The most entertaining battle between the righteous and the wicked is American politics, although it's probably more fun for me as an outsider looking in. It is easy to see the bad guy is in this one; the Republicans are the evilest group of people the world has ever witnessed. They are threatening over 7 billion lives; their tactics and greed supersede any evil entity in the history of humanity. They are obsessed with achieving the agenda of less government, less taxes for the rich, traditional values, and strengthened military at any cost.

Slavery is the most atrocious and utterly disgraceful act ever inflicted on a race of people; the Republicans are the descendants of the people who fought to preserve slavery. They are the party endorsed by the KKK, racists that make money at the expense of the lives of people. The Republicans have found a new kind of slavery, they have figured out how to legally enslave the poor. The average citizen works for food and shelter, with nothing left over, making them susceptible to life's intangible nature. Most every North American works to pay for shelter, gas, insurance, pharmaceutical needs; Republicans are influenced by these companies. Meanwhile, gas makes you sick, medicine helps your symptoms, and insurance pays for your hospital visit, it is quite a racket. These industries are running the world, and the laws reflect it, pollution standards for these companies drop whenever a Republican President is elected.

Republicans are loyal to their party, even if the leader is a liar, con-man, failed businessman, adulterer, or a moron. If he bans all Jewish people from the country, no wait, I meant all Muslims; they will still support their party. If it were the 1930s, Republicans would be marching all Muslims into death camps. Here in Canada, we take a more logical approach and make our decision for our counties representative of intellect and character, someone that I would be proud to represent me on the world stage. Being an American must be embarrassing when the Republicans are in power, not to mention the economic disaster that follows when it is the Republicans turn in office.

The lack of action by the republicans in Puerto Rico resulted in unnecessary deaths, the individuals who voted Republican also need to share in the responsibility in the deaths of these people. Actions have consequences, and if you voted Republican, then you are directly responsible for their actions. The people that died because of a weak response, killed because of prejudice. The Republicans don't pay the money out of their pockets; they didn't help because they are Puerto Ricans.

Republicans are generally heartless, so they have no problems being accountable for the deaths of six children, results of the Republicans plan to torture immigrants to detour them from trying to enter America at the U.S Mexican border. According to the U.S government, torture is an act committed by a person under the color of the law specifically intended to inflict severe physical and mental pain and suffering. That means the babies ripped from their mothers' arms, then locked in cages and are victims of crimes. I am surprised and saddened to see an internment camp in this day and age; I was under the impression that humanity was evolving. If you chose the Republicans to make government decisions for you, then you are also guilty of this heinous criminal act. To be clear, all serving republicans and everyone that voted for them are evil; even those who do have hearts, they are guilty by association.

There should be no debate on whether a glob of cells has rights, the fact is these cells are connected to the woman, and therefore by definition, it is not an individual. The woman with these cells attached to her has to make a responsible choice for the good of humanity. Imagine the improvement on society if every woman got abortions who knew they couldn't provide a loving home. The Republicans' stance on abortion is a veiled attempt to control women's bodies. They claim to be protecting an innocent life who cannot defend itself, but they have no problem flooding the streets with guns so that your child has his or her brains blown out on to their desk while they study at school. What if the shooter is the result of a denied abortion; in this instance, Republicans are killing your kids, and killing kids is evil. Unwanted pregnancies often end up to be burdens on society, and of course, they are against welfare and other social programs. They want small government when it suits them, except when it comes to the massive government over-reach of controlling women's bodies.

The Republicans are not above cheating in elections to fulfill their objective to lower taxes for themselves, outlaw abortions, loosening environmental standards for oil companies, and wage war. There are several instances where voting machines mysteriously malfunction in favor of Republicans; It would be idiotic to think that if they are evil, they would not cheat; that is what you would expect. I can't believe there wasn't a re-election when they cheated in 2016; the evidence is overwhelming. No less than six Republicans are convicted of crimes, committed to benefit their party. Some of the crimes they were found guilty of is conspiracy against the United States, tax evasion, bank fraud, campaign violations, witness tampering, obstruction, and identity fraud. I mean, if you rob a bank and don't get caught till a year later, you don't get to keep the money. Everyone knows that there are more bad apples in the Republican barrel.

A well-known tactic they use regularly is to accuse the other side of what they are guilty; they cast aspersions on the Democrats to deflect from their crime. They will bring up something unrelated to shift focus from the subject and never admit to any wrongdoings. Then the Republican-run news spins the narrative and does not broadcast anything that might hurt them; their audience is convinced that all other sources of news are fake.

The Republicans are the modern-day plague, but with much larger consequences, potentially murdering every son, daughter, mother and father on the planet. The crude oil they prize so much is dinosaur remains and after sucking up the dead's rotted carcasses that, after refined, is the fuel you burn in your vehicle or your house. Burning fossil fuel creates Carbon Monoxide, which is straight-up poison and is dangerously odorless. Entire families have succumbed to this deadly gas while asleep in their beds when it builds up due to poor ventilation. CO enters the bloodstream through your lungs and attacks your body at a cellular level. A contaminated cell becomes incapable of absorbing oxygen, as each cell dies, your skin turns pink, and you die. If you don't believe that Carbon Monoxide will kill you, please don't suck on a tailpipe to prove a point; the again, maybe natural selection will take care of some of the dead weight.

The circumference of the earth is 24,901 miles; the whisper-thin layer of atmosphere that encompasses the planet that contains enough oxygen to survive is less than five miles thick. I know this for a fact because Mount Everest is five and a half miles high, and the oxygen is so thin that people die from oxygen deprivation. Day after day, millions of engines burn precious oxygen and replace it with poison. This practice may have acceptable 100 years ago, but now that we understand how things work, there is no excuse. If you think carbon monoxide escapes into space, look at pictures of the smog hanging over Los Angeles in 1970. The ominous gray cloud that hangs over the city is proof that gravity holds oxygen, carbon dioxide, carbon monoxide, and other gasses close to the surface of the planet. Scientists estimate that humans are spewing 142 million tons of pollution a day into our precious layer of oxygen. We, as a society, are poisoning ourselves and the planet because we are too lazy and too stupid. Slow Carbon Monoxide poisoning is giving us cancer and other diseases by the millions. In 100 percent of cases of cancer, the common factor isn't smoking, every one of them has breathed air contaminated by Carbon Monoxide.

In North America, the two leading causes of death is heart disease and cancer; we would prevent millions of future deaths if we stop driving. Heart disease a thing of the past, eliminated because people get daily exercise going to work and the store. No matter what anyone says, motor vehicles are causing cancer, and it is utterly stupid to think otherwise. If carbon monoxide is responsible for those diseases, then what about Alzheimer's, Asthma and other environmental ailments. If you stop driving, the fracking will stop, no more wildlife destroying oil spills, and the end of air pollution from oil refineries.

You will be dead and buried before anyone admits that it is the vehicle exhaust that is causing these diseases. You can't expect that the ones taking in obscene amounts of money, not to say or do anything necessary to defend burning fossil fuel. When you cannot rely on the truth, you must use logic and common sense to make your determination. Cancer is precisely like getting Carbon Monoxide poisoning; it's just attacking the cells slower. When we breathe in Carbon Monoxide, our lungs distribute it throughout our bodies. Think about it; if the cause of cancer is not hereditary or communicable, then it is environmental. They use cigarettes as the scapegoat as the cause of cancer, but as humankind we have been burning plants since the discovery of fire with no legitimate cases recorded.

I hear people say that Cancer always existed but we didn't know what it was, but in 2018 there were 17 million new cases and the number increases each year. If you have ever watched a person die from Cancer, then you know how impossible it is to have existed in the past. Scientists can tell if a king was poison by Arsenic 100s of years ago; we would know if millions of people were dying in excruciating pain from their organs shutting down and their bodies bloating up. The wealthy are lining their pockets with oil, as coffin after coffin is lowered into the ground.

The only thing necessary for the triumph of evil is for good men to do nothing. We are about to enter into the most significant war humankind has ever had, the war to save humanity. In this war, you must not fear exercise and walk to the store or ride your bike to work in the service of your planet. You will face brutal hardships, and sometimes you will have to take a bus. In other words, you will have to give up the glory of owning a fossil fuel burning vehicle in order to save the human race. The government will never admit to how Carbon Monoxide is killing us because oil companies influence the government. The only way we can be saved, is to invoke change, this can only be achieved from action by the people. The time for talking is over, actions speak louder than words, you must take it upon yourselves to seize the opportunity to provide a future for your children. Once the polar caps are gone, the oceans will die and we will be unable to continue as a species. I want to believe our demise won't be because of our inept ability to take care of our home. As far as we know, we are beginning of life in the universe, and it is our responsibility to survive.

Tara's murder set forth a chain of events that brought me to this moment, her death was not meaningless and is yet to be determined the total relevance. My hope is this book might inspire another person to inspire another, and everyone accepts the accountability of being a human on this planet. Ask yourself if you on the side of good, will the world be a better place because you existed?

Chuck and Daisy

At this time I am not on social media, you can contact me at coolcuke.kk@gmail.com

www.ingramcontent.com/pod-product-compliance
Lightning Source LLC
Chambersburg PA
CBHW031114250726
48655CB00004B/1708